UPGRADE

YOUR MINDSET

LEADERSHIP LESSONS FROM LEADERSHIP SPECIALIST

ANTON GUINEA

First published by The Rural Publishing Company.

Copyright © Anton Guinea 2023.

eBook: 978-0-6458801-3-7
Print: 978-0-6458801-0-6

The Rural Publishing Company
Email: hello@theruralpublishingcompany.com.au
Website: https://theruralpublishingcompany.com.au

THIS IS THE MOST IMPORTANT BOOK DEDICATION YOU WILL READ.

This book is dedicated to all of those leaders out there who have never received leadership coaching. Who've never been supported to upgrade themselves. Who've never understood just how important it is to learn, grow, lead, in that order. This is the group of leaders who I wrote this book for. Don't worry, we've got you covered, if you're willing to come on a little journey with me to upgrade your mindset.

This book is also dedicated to old-school leaders. Leaders who didn't have to think about political correctness, who didn't have to think about offending people, and who didn't have to worry about raising their voices in meetings. Because you could do that in the 1900s. This is the other group of leaders who I wrote this book for. Never fear, we've got you covered, too, if you're willing to buy into the challenges of leading with heart and care factor, not just into taking an 'I'm not here to win friends' approach.

This book is dedicated to the teams that were impacted by the leaders mentioned above.

> **I was one of those workers, in one of those teams. I suffered through poor leadership, and I'm committed to helping the old-school leaders who are willing to learn how to think differently about leadership and about humans.**

Upgrading your mindset is thinking differently. It's about reacting differently. And, it's about responding differently. At its simplest, upgrading your mindset is about becoming reflective, so that you can answer the big questions about why you're a leader. At its more complex, upgrading your mindset is about knowing that every human is unique, every human is different, and every human has a very specific set of personal and professional needs.

If you read the paragraphs above, and you're a little freaked out, don't be. You have two options: you can put this book down and never look at it again, or you can work through it, and see what happens to your mindset, and to your approach to leadership. And see what happens to your team, and your team members, after you apply what you've learnt.

This book is also dedicated to all of the amazing mentors, coaches and trainers, who I've learnt so much from over the years. I've invested hundreds of thousands of dollars into my professional education, not only to be the leader that my team and business needs, but so I can share what I've learnt with you—the leader who's ready to upgrade their mindset!

Finally, this book is also dedicated to my amazing family, Mrs G (the amazing teacher), Toby (Son 1—engineer), and Zac (Son 2—future pilot) who've been on this crazy journey with me since 2004. They are my tribe, my number 1 team, and they are my motivation to be the best human and leader that I can be.

HOW TO USE THIS BOOK

This book is a playbook, not a story book.

It comprises a series of standalone ideas, elements, and tips and tricks to help you. It comes with actions to take to become a better thinker, a better leader, and a better advocate for your team's professional development. You'll also find a series of prompts and questions to encourage you to reflect honestly on your leadership skills and practices, and to think of ways to upgrade, upskill, and uplift yourself and your team.

Happy reading! You're on the way to being the best leader that YOU can be.

UPGRADE

YOUR MINDSET

WITH THE UPGRADE MODEL

This model was developed as a strategic tool for putting theory into practice to upgrade your mindset.

The model draws on various psychological theories relating to attitude, perception, and emotional experience in the workplace, and structures this information into a practical framework to guide leaders through the process of upgrading their mindsets to become better leaders.

It was developed over nearly 20 years of theoretical analysis combined with real-world experience, and it underpins the Guinea Group's winning formula for creating effective leaders, high-performing teams, and workplaces that are both physically and psychologically safe for workers.

Refer back to this model while reading this book. It'll help you form a concrete framework in your mind that will, over time, become a natural reference point as you grow and develop in your attitudes and behaviours, and move you closer to being the leader you want to be.

To make the most of this resource, contact us via our website at antonguinea.com.au for a self-diagnostic tool and action plan to review and improve your skills against the model.

01

START WITH A **FUTURE FOCUS**

Skillset: As a leader, decide who you're becoming

02

DEVELOP A **POSITIVE PERSPECTIVE**

Skillset: Practice the art of putting things into perspective

03

THINK ABOUT **YOUR THOUGHTS**

Skillset: Develop and practice the skill of introspection

04

LEAD **UNDER PRESSURE**

Skillset: Manage the pressure; don't let it manage you

05

KNOW YOUR **LEADERSHIP STYLE**

Skillset: Find your leadership style, and lean into it

CONTENTS

INTRODUCTION:
UPGRADE YOUR MINDSET

Upgrading your mindset is one of the most important steps to take in life. It can help you reach your goals, make better decisions, and become a better version of yourself. It can help you to become a better leader—as good a leader as those who've inspired you, or the leader you wished you had.

Changing your mindset isn't easy. It's a difficult job, and it requires dedication and hard work. It requires introspection.

But it it's worth it. Investing in it can help you become more resilient, confident, and happy—and a better leader for all the people who are looking to you for guidance and support so they can be their best, too.

This book was written for all of those leaders ready to upgrade their mindsets and move into the future as a better leader. It was written because so many leaders out there haven't received leadership coaching, and because so many don't even know that it's a thing. It was written because so many leaders don't understand that to be a better leader, they need to learn, grow, and then lead—in that order.

This book was also written because old-school leadership still exists. Even in this day and age, there are leaders who don't understand political correctness, and whose ideology and behaviour align with the problematic ways of leading we've been trying to let go of in the last decades. It was written because it's time for leaders to think differently about people and about leadership, and to lead with heart and care factor—because their teams need it to perform at their best.

Upgrading your mindset is how leaders can begin thinking differently. It's about reacting differently, and about responding differently. Throughout this book, I'll walk you through a process of instrospection, encouraging you to become more reflective so you can get to the core of the big questions about why you're a leader, and why you lead like you do. I'll encourage you to think about your leadership style, and how you can upgrade it to a style that allows you to be more resilient, better able to lead under pressure, and better relate to your teams—who need your leadership to perform at their best for you and your organisation.

Upgrading your mindset can be a complex process. But it's worth it—for you as a leader, and for the unique humans who make up the diverse teams you're leading.

Throughout this book you'll find activities, real-life anecdotes, and evidence-based leadership tips to help you upgrade your mindset. I encourage you to spend real time reflecting on what you're learning as you work through the book on your way to becoming a better leader—one with strength as well as care factor.

In the meantime, here's how you'll upgrade your mindset.

ONE IDENTIFY YOUR LIMITING BELIEFS.

The first step to upgrading your mindset is to identify your limiting beliefs. These are the beliefs that hold you back from achieving your goals and reaching your potential. Take the time to think about what these beliefs are, and how they're impacting on your life. Once you've identified them, you can start to challenge them, and begin to change them.

TWO SET GOALS.

One of the best ways to upgrade your mindset is to set goals. Having goals will help you focus your efforts and give you something to strive for. Make sure that your goals are realistic and achievable, and that they align with your values and beliefs.

THREE DEVELOP SELF-AWARENESS.

Self-awareness is key to upgrading your mindset. Take the time to understand yourself better, including your strengths and weaknesses, your values and beliefs, and your goals and motivations. This will help you become aware of how your thoughts and beliefs are impacting on your life, and help you begin to see how you can make positive changes.

FOUR PRACTICE POSITIVE THINKING.

Once you've identified your limiting beliefs and developed your self-awareness, it's time to practice positive thinking. Positive thinking helps to replace negative thoughts with more positive ones, which can help to upgrade your mindset by reframing the way you approach challenges.

FIVE TAKE ACTION.

It's important to take action to upgrade your mindset. If you find yourself stuck in a rut, or if you want to reach a goal, taking action is the only way to make progress. Make sure to set specific goals, and to put all of your effort into reaching them.

SIX SEEK HELP.

If you find yourself struggling to upgrade your mindset, it's important to seek help. This could be from a coach, a mentor, a therapist, or anyone else you trust. Talking to someone can help you identify any patterns or roadblocks that might be standing between you and your goals.

SEVEN DEVELOP SELF-DISCIPLINE.

Self-discipline is a key factor in upgrading your mindset. It's important to be able to stay focused and motivated, and to be able to push yourself to reach your goals. Developing self-discipline will help you stay on track, and to do what you need to do to get where you want to be.

By following these steps, you can upgrade your mindset and become the best version of yourself. It requires dedication and hard work, but the rewards are worth it. Upgrade your mindset today and take control of your life, and your leadership.

SKILL 1
START WITH A
FUTURE FOCUS

I WAS NOT A NICE HUMAN WHEN I WAS YOUNGER.

I was angry, I had a log (not a chip) on both shoulders, and I was very quick to escalate a conversation. From controlled to crazy out-of-control. Highly emotional. I had zero emotional control, and I didn't care.

When I reflect on being a younger man, and the less nice human that I was, I couldn't have told you what my mission was. After a lot of personal and professional development work, I'm now very clear on my purpose, and that is simply to leave people better than I found them. Simple, but a great driver of behaviour.

Back then, I was a tradie, so it didn't seem like a big deal. Everyone was like that. Or were they? There weren't too many on my crew that had the lack of emotional control that I did. But I made it OK. Until one day it just lost it. I had a massive stand-up blue in the workshop, with the boilermaker on our shift. It was so uncool! Let's just say that the language we used towards each other was colourful.

My lovely wife remembers the conversation that evening, and it was about me baring my soul and being brutally honest about my lack of people skills. I don't remember the exact words I used, but Mrs G remembers me saying that I was sick of not being able to get on with people, and that I was totally committed to changing my approach. And to learning new communication skills. But where do you start in this elusive quest for better connection with others?

With a future focus.

Mine started at Monash University, studying Engineering. Then I did a HR degree, and a postgraduate diploma at CQU. That'll fix it, I thought. The study was useful, and so was the work that I was doing on trying to understand humans. Understanding others was about watching and listening. Looking and learning. What made people tick? And what made them crack?

The journey has never stopped, and I recently completed a psychology degree. In saying that, the best thing I ever studied was NLP (Neuro-Linguistic Programming)—love it or loathe it, that program was an eye opener into the human species, and how we all connect.

Having studied people for nearly thirty years (I'm now doing a PhD in behavioural science), I share with leaders some of the simple techniques that they can use to improve their leadership and their connection. Especially when they're under pressure, which is the hardest time to connect.

Here are the three biggest lessons I've learnt about becoming the best human I can be (and failing plenty of times along the way).

ONE BE CLEAR ON WHO YOU WANT TO BE OR BECOME.

If you're happy where you are, stay there. But if you'd like to change something about how you behave, or who you are, decide what that new version of you looks like. Here's the challenge you'll face: if I asked you what your life's purpose is, you may or may not know that. 90% of the leaders that I ask this question to freak out and can't answer it. Which is cool. But if you can answer it, you'll be better placed to lean into behaviours that help you live your purpose.

If you don't know what your purpose is, the next best step is to understand how you'd like to be remembered. That's generally an easier thing to get your head around. Do you want to be remembered for the person that lifted others, or saw potential in others, or someone who was the toe-cutter or the Chief Twit? (Elon sacking thousands, as a case in point.)

When it comes to being remembered, I think back to all of the stories people have shared with me about their poor leaders. Some of those people share stories from decades ago, and how they still remember how bad those leaders made them feel. Yes, people remember conversations that hurt them, for thirty years and more. That's a long time...

LEADER ACTION

When you know what your purpose is (preferred) or at least how you want to be remembered, you can become the person and the leader who achieves that purpose.

TWO YOU REALLY DO NEED TO MAKE IT A PRIORITY.

Here's my next question for you: are you interested in or committed to becoming the leader that you want to be?

I see two types of leaders come through my programs. Type one went to university after leaving school. They move through their career, learning leadership on the job, spending three to five years at each level of the business, on their way to GM or CEO, and over time they become good leaders. Or not. Depending on the leaders that they're exposed to or the organisations that they join.

Type two leaders that I come across are those that do what it takes to become who they want to be. They get educated. They study humans. They stay in their leadership role for as long as it takes to master it. They know that it might take more than five years, or less, to develop the skills they need to progress their career. Some don't want to progress their career, they're happy at the level they're at, and they look for horizontal challenges and not vertical ascendance.

The thing that I know about leaders who become who they want to be is that they're clear on their direction. They do what it takes to get there. They sacrifice, they commit, and they dedicate themselves to the mission.

LEADER ACTION

Don't just be interested in becoming the leader you want to. Make it a priority and commit to it. Do something today to move you forward.

THREE BE COMFORTABLE WITH DISCOMFORT.

The challenge you'll face as you go after what you want to achieve as a leader is that you'll face trials and find yourself in uncomfortable situations. This is part and parcel of the growth and the development process.

This point reminds me of the great Australian world champion triathlete, @Chris McCormack.[14] When Macca turned up to race at the Ironman World Championships in Kona for the very first time, he was asked by the media if he was ready for the race. He scoffed, and said, 'Ready?...I'm here to win.' Which most people thought was a bit cocky at the time.

Macca couldn't even finish that race.

But he knew what he wanted to achieve, and over the next ten years, he turned himself into a three-time Ironman World Champion, and one of Australia's greatest ever triathletes. After all of that, Macca looked back over his career and wrote the book I'm Here to Win to honour where he'd come from in the very first race.

In that book, Macca wrote a lot about being able to 'embrace the suck.' In other words, being uncomfortable with discomfort. His theory is 'the person that can hurt the most during the race will win.' Just like leaders who develop themselves, getting out of your comfort zone and challenging yourself is part of the process of becoming an effective leader.

On the other side of discomfort comes growth. The more comfortable you can be with being challenged, the more you'll develop your leadership skills. And the better you'll learn to lead under pressure.

LEADER ACTION

Actively seek out opportunities to stretch yourself. Put yourself into positions or roles that challenge you and stretch your current skill set.

Having a future focus means deciding early in the journey who you want to become as a leader, and committing to making the changes that will be required for you to get there. It's also about finding opportunities to get out of your comfort zone on the way to becoming that leader and that human— and there will be plenty. Here's some of mine.

WHAT I LEARNT FROM DOING 700 LEADERSHIP COACHING SESSIONS

In January 2020, just before the pandemic whipped up its frenzy, Facebook started sending me ads for a thing called Remarkable. The metaverse must have been listening to my conversations (or maybe just my phone), and must have known that I write a lot, and that I've got piles of old books full of notes from meetings and coaching sessions.

The Remarkable looked cool, so I purchased one, and on January 24, 2020, I started documenting my coaching sessions in it, instead of in workbooks. Recently, I clocked over 700 coaching sessions, all documented in the Remarkable. Remarkable!

700 one-on-one coaching sessions, sitting with leaders at all levels of organisations, talking through their challenges or their wins. I've coached global managers and CEOs, and I've worked with team leaders. Both face-to-face and online. Either fortnightly or monthly, or weekly, even daily sometimes. Our coaching programs offer 24/7 support, which some leaders need at times. Some sessions take as little as fifteen minutes, but I've also spent full days with some leaders.

It's been a journey for me, and for the leaders I coach. The learnings on both sides have been amazing, and the conversations are documented, and sent out as part of the close out for every session.

In relation to my reflections, and the common themes that have come

through during those 700 sessions, here's three that stand out.

ONE LEADERSHIP CAN BE LONELY.

In our coaching sessions, I've seen (and experienced) every emotion, and then some. And what I've learnt about leaders is that things can change in a heartbeat. Life can be humming, and suddenly it gets uncomfortable. And, at times, lonely.

Leadership is such a rewarding experience for most, but at the same time, it can present such a challenge. And regardless of how much or how little support the leader is getting from their leader, there are times when leadership can cause feelings of isolation and loneliness.

Big decisions need to be made. Hard conversations must be had. All while there are teams and team members involved in and impacted by those decisions. It's so easy for a leader to say the wrong word, or use the wrong tone, or the wrong body language, and the relationship with a team or team member is strained for the next period.

My reflection is that leaders need a coach, and someone in their corner, who's external to the organisation, who they can talk openly to about their challenges. And of course, their wins. Don't worry, we celebrate success as much as we talk through issues, but at the same time, there's a confidentiality with coaching that makes it a hugely supportive process—where leaders feel like they've got a friend, as well as a coach.

My coaching on this is: if you find leadership lonely, reach out to a coach or mentor (or your leader), and be willing to have real conversations about your leadership and your team. These conversations will help you feel like you're not in this on your own. You're loved, and we're here for you when you need to chat. Life (and leadership) is a team sport.

TWO LEADERSHIP IS VALUES-BASED.

The clearer that leaders are on their values, the better results they get. Period.

Value alignment is such a key part of leadership because it's the thing that leaders go to consciously when they need to make tough decisions. Yes, our beliefs and conditioning drive our behaviour, but these are more subconscious, and we don't think about these too much (although we should do that, too).

Our values are the behavioural drivers that we go to when we're under pressure. If your value is honesty, you'll be driven by telling the truth. If it's caring, you'll lean into compassion and empathetic leadership. And if it's integrity, you'll be the leader who makes a commitment and follows through (not the one who commits and forgets).

My reflection on this one is that a lot of leaders haven't done a values exercise, and they aren't sure on their values, which makes it difficult for them. In several ways. Firstly, a leader's values need to align with the values of the organisation. It's not uncommon for me to hear a leader leave an organisation because their values aren't aligned with their business. This shows up with they're asked to do something that 'doesn't feel right.' Yes, leaders need to support business decisions, but at the same time, they'll feel challenged if how they're expected to behave is out of alignment with their caring value or their integrity value, for example.

My next reflection on this one is that if you ask someone about their leader, they'll generally talk in values-based words. So, our values are what we're remembered for. That's because values drive behaviour, and our behaviour is always on show.

And in case you're wondering, what's the one big overarching value that should drive leader behaviour? It's integrity. We've surveyed teams and asked them what they respect (and expect) from their leaders, and it's integrity. Which means the two elements of integrity—firstly, doing what's right, and secondly, doing what you said you would do.

THREE LEADERSHIP IS ABOUT CONTROL.

It's about control—in a good way, not in the power-hungry way. It's about internal control. Or more specifically, conscious control.

We get some great outcomes for the leaders that come through our programs, and I think the biggest compliment I could get is when leaders share that they have learnt the skill of 'responding, not reacting.' In other words, they've learnt to channel their emotional state, and breathe through the pressure of the situation.

Leaders that can create conscious control are able to control their behavioural responses. Which helps them control situations. And to control high-pressure situations. Which is when it's most important to be responsive, not reactive.

Emotional states are contagious. Leaders that can stay calm can help their team members stay calm. Some leaders I've coached have a poker face and try hard not to show when they're struggling emotionally. They try to 'shield' their teams from any pressure they might be facing.

The best leaders realise that their teams, and team members, are a reflection of their leader. If the leader is reactive, the team members will become that way, too. If the leader is in control, ditto (in general terms).

And again, in case you're wondering, one of the character traits that people are looking for from their leaders is consistency. Consistency means that the leader's emotional state isn't all over the place. It's consistent. Teams don't like working with leaders who are volatile or erratic. It's just uncool.

The other thing that rates highly from a team member perspective is care factor. Consistency and care factor are the two things your team is looking for from you, in relation to behaviour at least.

Finally, the very first coaching session that I recorded on my Remarkable was David Mallia on January 24, 2020. The 500th coaching session that I recorded on my Remarkable was Jayden Baker, on 5 September, 2022. If you do the numbers and count the working days during that period (670), then divide that by 500, you will get about 75%. So on average, I do three coaching sessions every four working days. That's between three and four coaching sessions every week—week in and week out.

It's been a blast, and my thanks and gratitude goes out to all the leaders that have trusted me to be in their lives. Their advice has helped support my future focus, and sometimes, even changed it.

But there's isn't the only advice that's helped. I've also gotten great advice in places beyond the profession, that's been just as invaluable.

THE BEST ADVICE I EVER GOT

The best advice I ever got was life advice from my favourite schoolteacher of all time. She's currently a grade six teacher. And I was never in any of her classes. I married her instead. This section is a shout out to Mrs. Guinea (as her students—and now, I—call her!), or Mrs. G for short.

When I met Mrs. G, she wasn't a schoolteacher. She was working in admin for the Queensland Police Service. Like me, she wasn't overly 'committed' at school. She didn't trouble the scorers when it came to report card time, and she's fairly open about the fact that school was more of a social affair for her (like much of her life still is). I was an electrician, and Mrs. G was a clerk. How things have changed in the 30-something years since we first met and fell in love and built an amazing life together.

Amazing for me—remember that Mrs. G married an entrepreneur—always a roller coaster ride for a supportive spouse. We've supported each other's goals over time, but I am lucky to say that Mrs G has always been there,

through the good and bad times in business, for which I am forever grateful. I sometimes say that I'm not sure how I got her to hang around so long. I'm glad she has, because she's taught me some amazing life lessons, and here are the best three (and if you're a leader out there, feel free to grab these and run with them—I do)!

ONE BE KINDER THAN IS NECESSARY.

This is my favourite Mrs G line of all time. Being kinder than is necessary is a great motto for life. It's about knowing what you should do, and then going above and beyond, because you care enough to. It's about paying it forward, it's about going out of your way to help others when you don't really have to. Or when you're not expected to. It's about smiling when you feel like frowning, and encouraging when you struggle to get the words out. It's about knowing that you don't like everyone, but you're still kind, regardless of the human you're dealing with.

TWO THEY WON'T REMEMBER WHAT I TAUGHT THEM.

Possibly the best line I have heard during my time on planet Earth. If you're a leader, they won't remember what you showed them; they'll only remember how you made them feel.

Mrs G steps into this and makes the effort with all her students. She's amazing at creating smiles. I love that about her, and about this advice.

I've taken this advice one step further, and in our business, my mission is to 'leave people better than I found them.' Many people have heard me say that in programs or in coaching. And if you ever hear me saying it, you'll know that we've got Mrs G to thank for that piece of wisdom—and for me, showing up with that as a goal and a life purpose is my 'why.'

THREE THERE'S GOOD IN EVERYONE.

The beautiful thing about this is that Mrs G really believes it, and leans into it. Because our beliefs drive our behaviour. How we think and feel shows up in how we act. When this is a strong belief, strong actions follow. One of the things that Mrs G is somewhat known for is being good with 'bouncy boys.' Aka, those boys that other teachers may not like to have in their class, due to how rowdy or excitable they can be. I love Mrs G's response to the question about how hard it might be to teach some of those boys—'I raised bouncy boys; they just need someone to see the best in them, to see their potential, and treat them accordingly. And they will blossom.' Isn't that beautiful? Go Mrs G.

Leaders, I apply these lessons as much as I can, especially when I'm under pressure. I hope they can help you out.

And if you ever see Mrs G, reach out and say hi! Love ya Jules.

HOW I SURVIVED A LEADERSHIP ROLE I WASN'T READY FOR

Having a future focus is important. It helps to reveal the steps you need to take to get where you want to go. But sometimes, you think you're ready for the next step, when you're not.

I thought I was ready. Some others (very few) thought I was ready. That is, ready for a demanding leadership role. But I wasn't. Not even close. But I took the role anyway. And pretty much failed.

CAN LEADERSHIP BE LEARNT, OR IS IT INHERITED?

Both. Leadership is a skill set. It can certainly be learnt. And it's inherited too (for the few lucky ones—studies have isolated the rs4950 genotype, the gift that nature has given some born leaders). I didn't get that gene...I've had to learn the hard way.

This really is the nature or nurture debate, and it's about how much of each is required for leadership. My theory is that you could be born with zero innate leadership abilities, but you can learn them—if you're committed enough. My experience is that most people aren't committed enough to doing the level of work that it takes to become a strong leader. Leadership learning is an important process. And it's a process that I didn't go through prior to taking on a high-stress leadership role.

I was a tradesperson. I could lead other tradespeople, right? Can't be that hard. I had a degree in human resources—that should have been all I needed to know, right? I was committed, and willing to work really hard and even do the work myself if I had to. That would get me through any difficult situation...right?

It should have pretty much been a NO to the three questions above. But I thought I was ready, and I thought I was right. Tip to young and future leaders: stop. Slow down. You've got heaps of time to build your career. I know you want that job tomorrow, but you don't need that job tomorrow. It'll come in time, when you're really ready for it.

No one could have told me, but if I could have been wise enough at the ripe old age of 29, when I got my first real leadership role, I would have read more. Watched more. Questioned more. Written more. And basically, I would have made leadership a study (not a university study, but a real-life study—which is what I'm doing now). And I would have gotten myself ready for the demands and the pressure of leading other humans, at least from a theoretical perspective.

During one of our leadership programs in 2021, we had a leader in a session who had been a leader for thirty years, who said 'It's great to be here, but I didn't know leadership training was a thing.'

WHAT HAPPENS WHEN LEADERSHIP GOES WRONG?

Yes, if you're reading this, and you've been a leader for a while, you'll say that no reading or training will set you up for the experiences you need to have as a leader, to develop your resilience, or your skills at leading with control, care factor, and courage. And you're right. Ish...

Leadership training and coaching does work. Some of my coaching is with future leaders, not just current leaders. And here is my experience from seventeen years of leadership coaching: future leaders are so much better at reflection and review than current leaders. Very few leaders spend time sitting, reflecting, reassessing and reinvigorating. Leaders, strangely enough, think that the experience itself will do the job for them. Just turn up, learn on the job, and we're all good.

That's when leadership goes wrong. Because leaders haven't learnt from the last time the same thing happened. And they keep hurting humans. Uncool.

And they let themselves lose control. Your burning question, like ours, should be 'why is important that I stay calm and in control as a leader, and how can I do that?' Tip to young and future leaders: reflect, review and reassess. And journal. Write stuff down. Commit to learning as much as you can about leading humans, and why it's so important.

But why, when leadership is the most important role on planet Earth—after parenting—don't we spend more time working on it?

Because leaders are too busy. Fun fact—most of my coaching sessions start with questions like:

Anton: G'day, how are you today?

Coachee: Oh, I'm so busy (or a derivative like busy, too busy, crazy busy, flat out, under the pump...etc).

Anton: How have you gone with your actions from the last session (which are usually about working on their leadership)?

Coachee: Scroll back up, and see the answer to question 1.

For me, I really have sympathy and empathy for the people I led in those early days. My apologies to all of them, and big thanks for being patient. It went wrong, a lot.

HOW DO YOU SURVIVE A LEADERSHIP ROLE YOU'RE NOT READY FOR?

I have no real pearls of wisdom as an answer to this question. In short, I bluffed my way through it. Mind you, I didn't bluff many other people. Poor leadership is usually glaringly obvious. Which it would have been for me.

And isn't that sad to say. There were humans involved. And I was bluffing. I had zero idea how to engage people, or motive them, at that time. Tip to young and future leaders: if you're in a role that you know deep down you're not really prepared for, please reach out. I'm here to help. And it's really OK to ask for help!

WHICH LEADERSHIP STYLE IS BEST?

Your style is best. As long as you can put your hand on your heart and say that you're doing the work, you're learning, and you're leading—on purpose. And doing no harm along the way.

And when you can also say you're working with a clear future focus—and you're actually doing the work it takes to get there.

WHEN IS NOW THE RIGHT TIME TO STOP PROCRASTINATING?

I've written 10,000 words of my next book. And they are great—really. But every time I go to write the rest of it, the fridge needs cleaning. Or I suddenly feel the urge to go for a run. Or a swim. Or to do anything else except book writing. Wednesday, Thursday, Friday (aka: WTF) is going on...

I'm being akratic, is what's happening. In other words, procrastinating. When we're under pressure constantly, we opt for easy and quick wins, instead of the important work. Beating procrastination is about self-discipline, and being in conscious control.

Firstly, let's go back in time to, oh, about 2,600 years ago, and unpack the origins of the word akratic, and how it's developed into what we now know as procrastination.

The concept of akrasia dates back to the time of the great Greek philosopher, Plato. Plato was perplexed (in the 300s BCE that is): 'why, if one judges action A to be the best course of action, would one do anything other than A?' Apparently, we procrastinated, even back then.

Aristotle also weighed in on the debate. He weighed in on things back then (before social media), and determined that the opposite to being akratic would be enkratic. Which was defined as having 'power over oneself.'

To top off the 4th Century BCE debate on why we don't get into action, we must go back to Socrates. Socrates must have been an action taker, as he's credited with founding Western philosophy. Socrates couldn't buy into akrasia, because for him, akrasia didn't even exist. His take on it was that 'no one moves willingly towards the bad.'

I wonder what Socrates would think if he was alive today, and he picked up one of the many books in bookstores on procrastination and how to get into action. I love his take on it, though—procrastination is moving towards the bad. Just knowing that might be enough to get some people into action.

And is procrastination moving towards the bad? Absolutely. Just think for a moment about how crapola (technical term) it feels to put things off day after day. And then imagining the intense pleasure and satisfaction that you would have felt if you'd stepped into that robust conversation, that book writing, that other-language learning, or the myriad other things that you would love to achieve but are putting off for some reason. I'm busy too. I get that. But we're not talking about a time issue here.

If it's not a time issue, then what is it? Why do we procrastinate?

Fear, generally. The fear of not doing it right (for the perfectionists). The fear of the response (for the people pleasers). Or the fear of the experience itself—like boredom from a long-term project (for the instant pleasure seekers). Procrastination can generally be attributed to one of these three, and if you can unpack the reason for yourself, you can get yourself into action, by doing one of the following—and these are a summarised version of tips from the great business philosopher (aka, author of Atomic Habits) @JamesClear[3].

ONE FIND A WAY TO REWARD YOURSELF SOONER.

The issue with procrastination, or what some people have termed the 'intention-action gap' (I prefer Akrasia, it just sounds cooler), is that there is a short-term reward. There's some instant gratification, that you use to make yourself feel better in the moment. But you sacrifice the feeling of satisfaction (which would be far greater) from doing the thing you're putting off. Find a way to reward yourself sooner for doing the hard things.

TWO HAVE SOME DISCIPLINE.

This is the conscious control piece. In the book Extreme Ownership by

@LeifBabin and @JockoWillink,[20] they talk about the word discipline. And what they mean is personal discipline. Personal commitment to a plan. Personal commitment to an action. Personal commitment to completion. In their world, discipline equals freedom. But discipline takes effort. It takes consistency, and it takes consideration of what your big goals (and small goals) are, and why they're important to you. Plan your days. Plan your weeks. Be disciplined with your time, and with your planning. Be on purpose. Ask yourself regularly, 'is this serving or sabotaging me?'

THREE LOOK ON THE BRIGHT SIDE OF LIFE.

This is the under-pressure piece. Pressure can push us towards negative thinking. We tend to (even in general terms) move by default to a negative. Or what might go wrong. 'What's the worst possible thing that could happen if I do this?' We blow up the negatives until they're huge—we think that 'I might not get it right', 'I could get ridiculed', or 'I have to do something that's rudimentary'. And those things might be true. What could also be true is the opposite of those, and the amazing positive outcomes and emotions that you'll feel, if you get it done. Focus on the positives and feel and see what could go right, not what could go wrong.

The great business philosopher (aka singer) @EricIdle nailed it when he shared with the planet the great advice to 'always look on the bright side of life'. Here are some of the lyrics from that song, which I think sum it up:

> I mean, what have you got to lose?
> You know, you come from nothing
> You're going back to nothing
> What have you lost? Nothing
> Always look on the right side of life
> Nothing will come from nothing, ya know what they say
> Cheer up ya old bugga c'mon give us a grin (Always look on the right side of life)
> There ya are, see
> It's the end of the film.

When you have the discipline and the attitude, the next part of future focus is putting it into practice—by dealing with other humans. For this part, you need more schooling, and it's learning emotional literacy.

LEARNING EMOTIONAL LITERACY

We're born. We go to school. We mature physically and sexually. We leave school. We go to work or university. And we think we've reached emotional maturation. Despite that we haven't learnt some of the fundamental skills of emotional control, and emotional channelling. And maybe never will.

In his book The School of Life—An Emotional Education, Alain De Botton explains that:

> **We aren't ever done with the odd business of becoming that most extraordinary and prized of things, an emotionally mature person—or, to put it a simpler way, an almost grown-up adult. In an ideal society, it would be not only children who were known to need an education. All adults would recognise that they inevitably required continuing education of an emotional kind and would remain active followers of a psychological curriculum.**

Firstly, though—what is an emotional education, or emotional maturity? An emotional education is one where we can put a name to the emotion we're experiencing. And we're self-aware enough at the time to do that. An emotional education is about being able to read the emotional states of other humans, and know what impact you're having on them, and why. It's about understanding that our moods matter, and that we (leaders especially) impact the emotional state of their team, just by the way we show up.

The universe is a mirror, and it reflects back to us what we put out there into the world. If you find yourself surrounded by people that are not always in a great emotional state, be brave enough to ask yourself the question of what contribution you've made to that. An emotional maturity will give you the confidence to know that other people's emotional states are not your responsibility, in general terms. But it's the confidence to know that if you're leading them, it's in your best interests to help them feel happier, rather than sadder, when they're at work. And that might take effort. To understand others, and to understand yourself.

Emotional maturity is understanding what your triggers are, and why you can't keep your emotions in check at times. We all have emotional triggers, and the emotional part of our brain fires within a second when triggers show up. Be prepared for triggers, and you'll be able to use your smart brain to respond, rather than react. You'll start to create conscious control.

Here are three things you can start doing right now to begin learning at emotional maturity school.

ONE REFLECTION.

As opposed to rumination. Reflection is about unpacking what happened (generally in a pressure situation), and what you can learn from it. It's a positive process that helps you to reframe a situation, and know that when faced with it again, you'll act in a more emotionally mature way. When we lose our emotional control, we can spend days (yes, days) ruminating on what happened, and why. We spiral negatively out of control, and it can make the situation worse. Or make it appear worse than it was or is. Reflection is a short process, that helps your subconscious mind to be prepared to do better in the future.

TWO INTROSPECTION.

The beautiful skill of going beyond reflection. Instead of just trying to understand how to behave differently into the future, introspection is about understanding how and why you process information in the world in the way you do. What are your belief systems? What are your values? Why do you do what you do, and what are your habits or patterns? What do you believe is acceptable, and what isn't? And why? These are big questions that most people never really consider.

THREE EXTROSPECTION.

The equally beautiful skill of not only understanding yourself, but also understanding others. Why do people do what they do? What must they believe to behave in that way? This is next level, and it takes that amazing skill of being able to read others while engaging with them at a deeper level.

With some reflection, some introspection, and some extrospection on a regular basis, you're back in school—the school of emotional control and emotional channelling. I say channelling very specifically, as emotional maturity is not about emotional suppression; it's about emotional direction.

Regardless of your emotional state, the goal always is to 'leave people better than you found them' (my purpose on planet Earth). If you use your emotional state to help, not harm, and to heal, not hurt, you're on a winner.

But working towards the future you're focused on isn't just about what you do for other people. It's about what they do for you, which is just as important. You can't make it on your own—you need to be ready to lean into help, even before you need it.

GETTING HELP BEFORE YOU NEED IT

I visited sunny Perth recently to speak at the *AusIMM Minesafe International Conference* and share some leadership insights with the mining community.

But there was one insight I didn't share in my talks, that I think is one of the most important of all: as leaders, especially in mining, we have to reach out and get help before we need it.

Let's rewind a little.

My mining career started at the ripe young age of 21. I was a young tradie who had just been released from a burns unit after more than a month of healing from a BOOM incident. I remember being in hospital and making the decision that I wouldn't be working as an electrician for any longer than I absolutely had to. That meant I needed to find something else to do with my career, and fast!

Within a year of starting work in the little mining town called Pannawonica in 1994, I heard about this thing called mines rescue. I was in. Probably for the wrong reasons at first, as I thought it might be a new career. But then, the enormity of the work dawned on me. And, not long after completing what felt like a decade (about two months) of training, I ended up as the captain of the mines rescue team on C Shift.

I was confident, but careful. I was focused, and fearful. I was alert, but anxious. I was the first port of call (with my team) for any incident that occurred on that mine site. A big role, with heaps of responsibility. There are so many roles on mine sites that can take their toll on people, and this is one of them. I was lucky, though...

I can still remember the two 190-tonne haul trucks crashing into each other, causing serious injury. The grinder that carved a path through Dave Partington's thumb. The head injury in the workshop after a fainting episode due to a fear of blood. The vehicle roll-over, that left two people badly hurt. And strangely enough I can still remember the insect in Ken McQueen's ear one night shift that we couldn't get out (that was a funny one). There were many more.

And knowing about psychology now, I know that these images (aka, episodic memories) get lodged in your hippocampus, neocortex, and amygdala. They start in your occipital lobe, and then get stored for later recollection. That is, whether or not you want to recall them.

My time in mining taught me that the terrible things you see (and feel) in life don't go away. They stay with you. And since that time, I've really understood how PTSD occurs. I get it. Big time. There must be a point when there are too many images and memories in there. And it gets too much.

And that would be the same for leaders, not just mines rescue team leaders. Mining can be pressure packed. I'm lucky that I had people around me to help. The secret for me, was to reach out and to debrief quickly after the incidents. To be open and honest about what I felt, which despite my youth, I actually was able to unpack.

Until (and sorry, don't read on if you're squeamish) the day I was playing football with Mick Fursman, when his foot turned around and was left facing the wrong way. Horrible. In that moment (and sorry Mick) I said, 'sorry mate, you're on your own,' and I had to walk away. I resigned from mines rescue straight away, and never attended another incident. To this day, blood and gore I can handle, but body parts out of place...that's really not OK.

I wonder if I really did reach out enough prior to that incident, or if it was fate. Who knows. But as a leadership coach, my advice is to reach out for support before you need to, and don't let one incident stop you from reaching the future you're focused on.

LEAN INTO MEN'S HEALTH

Recently, I was lucky enough to share some of my insights into men's mental health at a men's circle event at Agnes Water. The issue of men's mental health is a major issue in Australia: a LOT of men die by suicide each year in this country. And we need to do something about it.

I shared my experience of having a serious workplace incident, and the impacts that experience had on my life. The good, the bad and the ugly. I shared what 100 days of anxiety looked like for me, and how hard that process was. From the seeing a doctor for a script, and not getting it filled, to talking myself through the process.

Recently, and maybe since I've turned 50, I've started to feel compelled to share more of my experiences and challenges, in the hope that others might just learn something from my story. Although, in general terms, I've been very blessed in my life, there have been one or two little hurdles along the way that have been very difficult to deal with. And without my supportive wife and kids, the stories might have been different.

With 44% of Australians being diagnosed with a mental health condition in their lifetime, it's important to lean into men's mental health and make it OK for men to open up to others—not just so you're equipped to keep on tracking toward your future, but for resilience throughout your whole life.

But I don't think men have trouble sharing their feelings. What I think the problem is, is that other men aren't good listeners, and they don't hold the space. They try to fix stuff up. That's not supportive.

Here are some things that I would share with men everywhere to help them reach out when they need to.

ONE BE VULNERABLE.

When I talk to groups about any topics, including mental health, I try to provide practical advice and tips that can be implemented straight away.

Topics like being vulnerable are very broad topics. And most people can describe what it means to share your inner struggles with another human—even if it means that they know deep personal stuff about you—but it's harder to actually practice it.

Vulnerability takes a whole lot of courage for men. This is about exposing your underbelly and giving people information about you that they could share or 'use against you' in the future. Which is what one man in the men's circle said was his biggest issue with sharing personal information.

LEADER ACTION

The action, or the process, of being vulnerable always starts with words like 'I am feeling', 'I feel like', 'I am experiencing', 'I am hurting', or…'I need someone to talk to'.

TWO BE EMPATHETIC.

Vulnerability is for the person speaking, whereas empathy is for the person listening. Listening with care factor.

Empathy is about stepping into the same emotional experience that the other person is having. Which is very achievable for any man, if they're willing to make the effort. There are times when empathy starts at sympathy, which is a natural response, and in those cases, it's easier to feel what someone else is feeling.

There are times though, when you need to come to empathy from apathy (low care factor) because their challenges don't seem big enough. That's where the real effort comes in. And that's OK.

LEADER ACTION

The action, or the process, of being vulnerable always starts with words like 'thanks for trusting me', 'thanks for sharing', 'congrats for being courageous', or 'I'm here for you'.

THREE BE PRESENT.

To me, this is the most important skill set, when it comes to supporting someone who's struggling. Being present means being in the conversation. It means holding the space (thanks, Brene Brown). And it means keeping your mind focused on not only the words being said, but also the message behind them.

Being present is a little like leadership listening, when you're listening to understand, not to respond. And yes, if you think back to empathy, it's nearly impossible to be empathetic if you're not present.

Presence can mean not even talking at times. It can be just sitting with someone who's hurting. It can be about just being there. If the person has things to share, it's about lingering in the conversation. Not changing the topic, not deflecting. Being available.

LEADER ACTION

The action, or the process, of being present is simply about 'tell me more', 'talk me through it', 'what I'm hearing is...'

Every man has a story. And at some stage, they'll need someone to listen to it. If you ever need to share your story, find someone you trust, and be vulnerable. If anyone ever needs to share their story with you, be empathetic and be present. Our futures depend on other people.

ACTIVITY 1.1
START WITH A FUTURE FOCUS

Take some time now to think about what you've learnt in the last chapter.

The series of questions on the following pages will encourage you to think about who you want to be or become, and to apply the lessons you've just learnt in developing a future focus to the process of upgrading your leadership mindset.

I encourage you to answer the questions, but if you find this activity doesn't work for you, consider journalling. It's also a valuable use of time just to sit and write about your values, your goals, and any challenges you need to tackle in your leadership role.

Who do you want to be or become?

Are you prepared to be 'comfortable with discomfort' through the process of working towards who you want to be as a leader?

In what ways could you make upgrading your leadership mindset a priority?

What are your primary values? Do they align with the values of your organisation?

How do you think your leadership makes your team feel? Can you think of ways to improve this?

List some good character traits or behaviours in your team members that you value. Can you think of ways you could show your team that you value them?

Do you leave people 'better than you found them'? If not, can you think of ways to improve this?

Can you think of ways to become more vulnerable, more empathetic, and more present in your leadership?

SKILL II

DEVELOP A

POSITIVE

PERSPECTIVE

Is the World *Really* Going to Implode? Or Could You Put Things Into Perspective?

Could you put things into perspective, and understand that this pain or situation is temporary? And that emotional control is more important than blowing this situation out of proportion?

Leadership is so lonely at times. You feel like you've shattered a mirror, been cursed by a black cat, or walked under a ladder. Every day. Forever. And it never stops. Right?

Leadership pressure comes in so many forms. From so many directions. How we respond (or react) to that pressure is often about the perspective we've chosen to take.

Perspective taking is not a new topic. Around 500 BC, the Greek Philosopher Heraclitus talked about the difference between appearance and reality, where nothing ever simply 'is' but is 'becoming' something else.

In 2020, we call that perspective taking. What are we experiencing? Could it be interpreted as something else? Something less stressful, something less dramatic? What could it become if we responded differently?

For some leaders, perspective taking comes easier than for others. Why can some leaders stay calm under fire, and others struggle to keep it together? Is it genetics, or our nature? Or is it our experiences, our nurturing? Nature or nurture? Or both?

I say both.

We know that some people are born more pessimistic than others. And some are more optimistic than others. Regardless of how you look at the glass of water, it either has water in it or it doesn't. Look at a 9 upside down and you'll see a 6.

In a previous life, I was a maintenance superintendent, which meant I was responsible for the maintenance in an industrial plant. I would freak out—literally—when the plant broke down. Every time I got a call about a breakdown, I would turn it into a catastrophe of epic proportions.

After about eighteen months of stressing about keep the plant running, I looked to my manager for coaching and advice. He never seemed to get stressed like I did. One day, he explained that he'd been in the Navy. The aircraft carrier that he was on was bombed, and suffered substantial fatalities and casualties. He shared that plant breakdowns are not life and death events. 'When my life was in danger, I got stressed. Nothing much seems to stress me anymore', he said.

We teach perspective taking in our training and coaching. It's about the three elements of turning the problem around, to look at it differently (1). Then, engaging with others (2), to get their perspective. And then, languaging it differently (3), and reframing the problem or the situation.

The next time you're stressed, try those strategies. Don't thank me now!

HOW'S THAT WORKING OUT FOR YOU?

What a great question. And one that I ask my leadership coaching clients all the time. To work out what they're doing that's not serving them. And to work out why they persist with whatever it is that's not working. Especially if the leader is not getting the results that they want.

And don't worry, I have to ask myself the same question sometimes. I usually don't like the answer. Because although doing the same thing and expecting a different result is the definition of insanity, the human species is persistent. We don't give up easily, and we persist even when it's time to take a different approach.

As you read this, make it personal, and think about a behaviour you'd like to change. Something that you're doing, and doing again, that's not getting the results you desire.

Firstly, why do we persist doing things that don't serve us? There are three reasons:

ONE THE SIMPLEST IS BECAUSE NO ONE EVER CALLS US ON IT.

And we don't call ourselves out on it.

Hominins are habitual creatures. And from a neurological perspective, habits are just neurons that have been wired together to form a behavioural pattern that's easy and consistent. Even when we aren't getting the results we expect. Until we can break the neuronal connections. Literally. For this one—get a confidante.

TWO NEXT, WE HAVE A RANGE OF LIMITING BELIEFS.

We'll continue doing the same thing, because 'it's the way it's done', or 'that's the only way to fix this'…all while we continue to live in hope that something will change. We might even think that it's too hard to change, or that we're not good at the thing we're trying to achieve. For this one—get reflective.

THREE BECAUSE THERE'S SOME SORT OF REWARD OR INTRINSIC BENEFIT FROM THE BEHAVIOUR.

As much as we don't want to admit it, there is an upside to every behaviour pattern. Even if it's just a time saver or if it gives us something to complain about, we don't do things that don't serve us in at least some small way. Think addiction. Even addictive behaviour has a pleasure part to it. We're motivated towards pleasure and away from pain (even it if is short term). For this one—get a coach.

SECONDLY, WHAT WILL IT TAKE TO MAKE LASTING CHANGE?

Generally, this question can only be answered with an understanding of your ability to change (knowledge and skills to develop an updated behavioural process) and your willingness to change.

The skills part is an easy one. A leadership coach (or a confidante in your team) can assist with this one. Or do some training. Or just Google it. Skills and knowledge can be learnt. But knowledge is not knowledge without action. You don't know something if you're not applying it.

If someone asks you 'how's that working out for you?' that might be enough for you. Here's a better question to ask if you're not getting the results you want from the behaviour patterns and habits you're running: 'In relation to this issue—are you interested in changing or committed to changing?'

The answer to this question will tell you all you need to know about why you're persisting with a behaviour that isn't supporting you or getting you the results that you're chasing. And it can change not only the behaviour, but the perspective you take from then on—a more positive one.

HOW I GOT OUT OF MY DEPTH TOO QUICKLY

BOOM!

You're a leader, and you've just had a catastrophe. The economy has blown up. The plant has blown up. Your life has blown up. What do you do?

Here are the three most common responses from leaders whose existence has gone BOOM at some stage. And a fourth one, where humans are the key concern.

ONE THE FREEZE-AND-FREAK-OUT RESPONSE.

Yes, an extra F word in there (and it's not fight). Some leaders are like the proverbial deer in the headlights. In Australia, it's like driving down that outback country road at sunset and a large kangaroo is sitting in the middle of the road and hasn't got a clue that the lump of metal coming towards isn't a light of truth, but a kangaroo-killing machine. But it freezes anyway, not knowing what to do. There's a fear response too, especially as the car gets closer. But it still can't move—it's frozen in place.

Its stress response keeps it glued to the spot. To its detriment, usually. For humans, when the BOOM is too much, we don't know which way to turn, and what action to take. So, we do what the kangaroo does.

Until someone drags us into a meeting, or needs our support, or needs something else from us. Basically we freeze, until a human shows up, and the human is a reason to get into action.

LEADER ACTION

Pull yourself out of the freeze- or freak-out response, take the lead, step into the BOOM situation, and work through it. With the help of others. And to help others. Because humans are the key concern. Always.

TWO THE FIGHT-AND-FEND-OFF RESPONSE.

Yes, another extra F word in there (and it's not flight). Some leaders get aggressive at the first sign of pressure. They go on the attack. As well as getting aggressive, they can tend to get abrupt and abusive.

They act like what Australians call a bungarra lizard (a 2-metre long prehistoric sand lizard). If you've ever lived in the bush, you get warned about bungarras. Never corner a bungarra, is the warning. Because if you do, they only know one way out, and that's to run straight up and over you. And they need their sharp claws to climb, and apparently—so the warning goes (not sure how true it is, but I don't want to try it)—they climb well. And fast. Straight up your body.

A bit like what some leaders do, under pressure.

Until someone has the courage to call them on their behaviour, and gets them to check themselves, and their response to the BOOM.

LEADER ACTION

Understand that the humans around you are feeling the pressure too, and that they need to be supported and cared for. Create a safe space, and become more compassionate and empathetic. Because humans are the key concern. Always.

THREE THE FLIGHT-AND-!@#K-OFF RESPONSE.

Yes, another extra F word in there (and it's a bit naughty—but every book I pick up these days has it on the cover, so it must be OK). Some leaders become invisible when the pressure is on.

They seem to disappear into the night and reappear when the BOOM is over, or the work is done. A good strategy for their own self-preservation, but not great for their team, who need them more in those moments than most others.

These leaders are a little bit like the Australian wild horses. Who can sleep standing up. This is an evolutionary thing, and like a human flight response, a horse can go from sleeping to galloping in no time flat. Evolutionarily, the horses that could flight (or f-off quickly) survived longer than horses that slept lying down, who were easy prey for carnivores. That strategy is a winner for wild horses, but not great for leaders.

Until someone calls the leader out on their aloofness and asks for support or help, leaders flight off, and for whatever reason, think that's OK. I can remember as a young tradesperson, being alone on a job at night, at the end of shift, with no leadership around, not having a clue what I was doing. It was the leaders that stayed and helped that I respected the most.

LEADER ACTION

Don't flight off. Stay back, and offer help, even if you're anxious and don't know what to do yet. Because humans are the key concern. Always.

FOUR THE CARE AND CONNECT RESPONSE.

Or, as psychologists term it, tend and befriend.

To care and connect is to be a good leader. And a good human. When things go BOOM, you can't do it all on your own. You don't have all the answers. You don't need to. You have a team that know more than you (collectively) in relation to the correct response. They just need to be listened to and heard.

During a BOOM event, care factor is the most important element of any leader response. Leaders who demonstrate care factor keep their emotions in check. They take charge of the situation, and they make sure that their teams have a safe place to work from. They create what is called 'psychological safety', and they create a safe place for others to step up and be part of the response effort.

LEADER ACTION

Take charge, create a safe place for others to offer help, then thank those people for their efforts. Because humans are the key concern. Always.

These responses are the result of your perspective. If you can move towards developing a positive one, you'll be more likely to respond by caring and connecting—which will help to positively influence the person you're responding to, and further improve your own perspective with the positive benefits it brings to both of you.

How To Develop Your Relationship With Failure

During 2002, I was in charge of the maintenance of an industrial plant that was part of a smelter in New South Wales. It was 3 p.m. on a Friday afternoon. I'd done some calculations to determine how much bolt tension should be applied to the bolts in the pipework of a critical part of the plant.

So, when one of the team was tightening up the bolt and asked if I was sure that he should tighten it to what I had calculated, I said very confidently, of course. The problem was that I'm not a mechanical engineer. I had an electrical background, so I wasn't really the right person to be doing those calculations in the first place.

When the fitter tightened the bolt (based on my incorrect calculations), it cracked the cast iron pipework. Which meant that the plant couldn't go back into service. The pipework was an odd shape, and it couldn't be weld-repaired. It had to be rebuilt from scratch. Which would take between 24 and 48 hours, due to the manufacturing process required.

In short, the plant was then out of service for the time that it took to obtain a new section of pipe, to repair the damaged one. The material cost of that mistake was hundreds of thousands, if not millions, in lost production. Not a small loss for that business. And not a small failure on my part.

To this day, that decision rates as probably my worst failure in the workplace. The most expensive, at least. And probably the most embarrassing. Because if someone better qualified than me had have done the calculations, they would have allowed for the stress point in the pipework, where there was a spacer (it wasn't flat pipe on pipe, that the bolt was doing up).

And you know the old saying that you don't get remembered for the good things you do, only the one failure? That's what happened in this case. It was tough. In the end, it happened, and I was up all night (which was common at that workplace) working with the supplier to get the pipe rebuilt.

After plenty of thinking and feeling bad about that incident, here's what I learnt about dealing with failure, and how your response to it can shape a more positive perspective into the future.

ONE RESIST RUMINATION.

Rumination, as opposed to reflection, is overthinking what happened. Going over it in your head with a negative perspective on the incident. Talking yourself down and giving yourself a hard time about how silly you were, and how badly you performed. And how badly others are going to think of you. Rumination is negative self-talk, and it keeps you stuck in the past.

Reflection, on the other hand, is more of a positive review of what happened. With a forward focus. Develop the mindset that failure is OK, it's part of life, and it happens. If you're out there trying new things, that is. Reflection is about knowing that you are OK as a human. Knowing that your intent was right, and you didn't mean for this situation to occur. It's about being gentle on yourself and knowing that you'll find a way (with a future focus) to prevent this same thing from happening again. Reflection helps you learn about what went wrong, and why.

In my experience, this is the toughest thing to do. To change your thinking from how bad the situation is, to what you could learn. Reframing is a skill that can help here. It took me months to feel better about the pipework failure. When I got the lesson, though, which was that I should have gotten some support with the technical decisions I was making, I felt better.

From a psychological perspective, reflection is the key skill that will let your subconscious mind know that you're ready to deal with a similar situation in the future. Subconsciously, you'll have a level of fear or anxiety about the situation, and that fear can destroy your confidence. Because your subconscious will keep you from being in a similar situation, because you aren't ready to deal with it. Until you get the learning from the failure, that is!

The questions you should be asking yourself to help you reflect should be around what you can learn from the situation.

TWO OVERT OWNERSHIP.

Dealing with failure is about taking ownership for what happened. Overt ownership is not simply reporting the failure or sharing it with your leader. It's about completely and openly owning it.

By doing what it takes to make the situation right. If it can be made right.

This is the one that I see too often as a coach. People going to their leaders thinking they've taken ownership by admitting or 'owning up to' a failure or a mistake. This is completely not overt ownership. To me, this is covert ownership. That is, thinking you're taking ownership, but really you're just handing the issue over to someone else. Uncool.

Overt ownership means doing everything in your power to remedy the situation. Fixing the issue. Addressing what happened. Not giving it to someone else to fix.

The upshot of overt ownership is that you feel way better about the situation because you're getting into action. And you go to your leader with the action plan, not the failure or the mistake. It makes for a different discussion. A discussion with a more positive spin. I went on the journey with the manufacturer and worked day and night (literally) to make sure that the pipework was repaired as soon as it could be.

The questions you should be asking yourself to help you take overt ownership are around what you can do to address the situation, and to repair any issues that have been created.

THREE FUTURE FOCUS.

Having a future focus is really the outcome of resisting rumination and overtly owning your part in the failure or the issue. Having a future focus is about focusing on what you're going to do differently moving forward, and into the future.

From what you've learnt, and from what you've done to rectify the situation, it's then a matter of where to from here. What are you going to change in your behaviour or your decision making that will ensure that you don't let the same thing happen again?

Having a future focus starts right now. In this very instant. Get into action. Being on purpose. And knowing that into the future you won't make the same mistake because you've changed your thinking or your processes to set yourself up for success.

For me, this was a matter of ensuring that I put processes in place to get the technical support I needed, when I needed it. The questions you should be asking yourself to support a future focus are around what needs to be put in place to prevent recurrence of the issue.

So, how do you develop your relationship with failure? Learn from the situation, do what it takes to rectify it in the moment, and think about what you need to do to prevent the same thing from occurring into the future.

Failure is normal. It doesn't define you. And a positive perspective of it can bring the learning you need to change your future for the better.

HOW TO RETAIN YOUR TOP TALENT

2020 was the year of lockdowns and working from home. 2021 was the year of the great resignation. 2022 was the year of quiet quitting. 2023 was the year of moonlighting (or even career cushioning), or supplementing your income from another source. None of these options are good for your business, or your productivity.

But what can you do to be proactive, and to ensure that your top talent stays on? And stays because they want to—not because they have to, to take a pay cheque—but because you give them a good reason to?

It's all about perspective. If you want to retain your top talent in the 2020s, here are some top tips.

ONE EMBRACE FLEXIBILITY.

Remember again for a moment that it's the 2020s. Old-school organisations and old-school leaders are not going to be successful anymore. Even though 89% of organisations are following Elon Musk's lead and adopting a voluntary separation process (Credit: Spiceworks.com), or voluntary redundancy, as you might know it, the underlying issue is that it's not the under-performers who are leaving, it's the top talent.

Because they can get a better deal elsewhere (rightly or wrongly). Because their expectations have increased (which is OK). Because their leaders aren't adapting and developing a 2020s workplace (which is absolutely happening right now).

I feel like the next 2–3 years will see the landscape of working arrangements settle down and go back to the pre-pandemic office-based practices. Or organisations will shift their thinking to a post-pandemic mindset. One or the other will become the norm, but for the moment, flexibility is key, if you want to retain top talent. If your top talent wants to work from home for some of their working hours, or they want to work different hours, or they want to work compressed hours, have the conversation, and listen to why these are important to your team members. These changes may not all be practical, but they should at least be heard, and considered.

TWO TEAM MEMBERS DON'T LEAVE ORGANISATIONS. THEY LEAVE LEADERS.

Sadly, leadership growth has not moved at the same trajectory as employee flexibility has. Or articles like this would not be a thing.

Some senior leaders are inspired by layoff programs and processes, like the way it was done at Twitter. Cut the dead wood and move on. And this is completely necessary at times, but at the same time, the more poorly handled the layoff process is, the more difficult it is for top talent to feel confident that they're not going to be next in the firing line.

Remember that other global organisations have undertaken mass layoffs, but they haven't been as public. Why? Because they were done in a more people-centred way. And that is too boring to make the news. The more professional the process, the less fanfare.

I feel like leaders are still reeling from the past 2–3 years. I know that they should have embraced and moved on, but the pandemic was such a disruptive force that leaders feel like it should be done and dusted now, and that things should go back to how they were. When they probably never will. Leaders that are unwilling to listen, that aren't embracing psychological safety, that aren't leaning into people over production, will retain their positions. But they won't retain their top talent.

THREE CARE FACTOR.

Teambuilding.com recently listed the top eleven things that organisations can do to address the challenge of quiet quitting.

I feel like this is the best list of things leaders can do, although a list of eleven could be seen as long and arduous. I will list the ten things below, but if you like my summarised version of them, it'll increase your care factor, and help you think about what team members need to feel engaged at work. What they need to feel cared for. What they need to feel valued at work.

If you're a leader, and you feel like your team is quietly quitting, try to keep increases in workload short-term. Properly compensate and remunerate your team members. Make stepping up optional, and be upfront about future role growth. Lean into employee recognition strategies, and at the same time, try to monitor mood and behaviour changes. Encourage breaks, and support employee wellbeing. Build rapport and relationships, while maintaining boundaries to promote a work life balance.

Whatever you call it, the great resignation or quiet quitting, if your top talent is leaving, it's time to intervene. Changing to a more positive perspective with flexibility and care factor will change theirs, too.

FALSE EXPECTATIONS APPEARING REAL

Crapola perspectives lead to crapola feelings, and to crapola behaviour.

Recently, I had an experience that scared the crapola out of me. And there was no real need to experience that fear (aka: false expectations appearing real). I thought my life was in danger, literally.

Here's what happened, and why it's so relevant for us in business, and life.

This year, I'm climbing Mount Larcom as many times as possible. Aiming for fifty, but may not quite make that. I'm working hard on it. I'm up to twelve for the year. It's a 3.3-kilometre climb, and it's far from easy. It takes around 1.15 hours to get up and a little less to come down. And due to my other commitments, I generally start climbing at crazy o'clock. Most starts are between 3 a.m. and 4 a.m.

Recently, I was walking along the trail, and it was pitch black, other than my head lamp. And apart from the toads croaking and the leaves rustling, there wasn't a lot of noise or action. Until, suddenly, and unexpectedly, I looked up and saw a human in front of me. Sitting on a rock, on his phone. No head lamp, pitch black, just sitting there. Scared the heck out of me.

'I don't see people here at this time of the day,' he said. I replied, 'me either.' As I kept walking. Nearly running by this stage.

Just imagine. Pitch black. Out in the middle of the bush, half an hour out of town. And only two of us on the mountain. One of those humans now walking like he was being chased. Which I wasn't. But your mind goes all over the place, seriously. I was wondering where he would bury my body. Every noise I heard, I thought it was him coming up behind me. I kept stopping to look back, straining my eyes to see if I could see him coming. I remembered the stories about backpackers being murdered and tried to remember what the survivors did to get away from their attackers.

I was seriously next-level freaking out. It was a fear I have not experienced probably ever.

And then, when I was coming back down the mountain, I saw this card that was left on a pile of rocks that said, 'You are saved.' I doubled down on the fear levels. I was saved—from what? Being dumped on a mountain, never to be found or heard from again?

And you know what? All I could think of was that I might have even turned about and not gone up the mountain that day if I saw that person earlier.

But here's the thing. I know that the person I saw was just doing his thing. He wasn't there to harm me, or anyone else. He probably didn't even leave that card on the rocks. And when I got home and told my family I was lucky to be alive, and showed them the photo, it turns out the card said, 'You are loved.'

I worked myself into a dither that morning. I was so scared. And all that fear was totally unjustified. There was nothing to fear. It was my imagination. False expectations appearing real. And to think that I might have turned back just because there was another human there early in the morning.

I've thought about this story a lot since it happened. And wondered how much I (we) have let fear stop us acting. How many times have we turned around instead of tackling a challenge head on? How many times have we focused on what might go wrong instead of what might go right? How many times have we created expectations that were imagined?

Too many, would be my answer to the questions above.

And the message is to turn Fears into Pears—positive expectations appearing real. Imagine how good it'll be to get to the top of your next mountain climb! And how much better that will feel?

HOW TO ELEVATE YOUR LMX

The quality of a leader will be determined by the quality of the exchanges that they have with their team members (also known as Leader Member Exchange, or LMX). And this is heavily influenced by perspectives on both sides of the exchange..

LMX as a theory has been researched widely since 1975, but if you haven't heard of it, you're not alone. If that's the case, this bit's for you.

When I say elevate your LMX, what I mean is to increase the quality of the communication and connection that you have with all team members. Not just those who you trust the most, or who you rely on the most.

Let me give you the short version first. LMX is about a reciprocal exchange between leader and team member. Reciprocal being the operative word— meaning here, a two-way exchange, that's about an elevated level of dialogue. Honest. Open. Candid. A two-way dialogue based on a degree of mutual trust, loyalty, support, respect, and obligation. The concept was developed by Fred Dansereau, George Graen, and William Haga.

What is also important about LMX is simply that higher quality LMX leads to a growth- and development-focused relationship (for the team member), and lower LMX is associated with less team member growth (and subsequent growth opportunities). Higher LMXs result in career conversations. They result in idea generation sessions. They result in candid (reciprocal) feedback sessions. They result in a more developed relationship.

Please read this paragraph carefully, as this is the most important, and probably the most honest, element of LMX theory. It says that leaders have a subconscious rating process, where they (we) make a subliminal judgement call about each and every team member.

Team members (unknowingly, and unwittingly) end up in the 'in-group' or the 'out-group'. And yes, leaders (we again) treat these two groups of team members differently. Yes, we are only human, but it's good to know how this works, and what you can do to make sure you're more conscious with your leadership, and that you take an LMX approach to your conversations. With a positive perspective, and not just writing team members in or out.

Here are the three parts of LMX explained.

ONE ROLE TAKING.

No matter how much you read about LMX, there's never much written about this part of the process. The line is generally 'this takes place when a new

member joins a team, and their abilities are initially assessed by the leader.'
And I get that it's a simple process, but there must be more to it than just
that one line.

I think about the Tuckman model, where teams go through forming,
storming, norming, and then performing. And every time someone
joins a team, the team will go back into forming stage, regardless of the
characteristics of the new team member. Some team members fit in, and
some don't. Right? So, the storming stage might be longer or shorter, based
on the team member. And potentially how well the new team member gets
on with the leader.

Yes, a leader does make an initial assessment, but if you're reading this,
remember that leaders do change their minds. It's not all bad news if you
get put in the out-group from the outset (that's my take on it, at least).

TWO ROLE MAKING.

Role making is what happens after leaders categorise their team members.

Team members who are subconsciously added to the in-group are trusted
more. They're given more growth opportunities. In short, these team
members experience a better relationship—and, dare I say it—treatment
from their leader. Conversely, team members who are subconsciously added
to the out-group are not communicated with as openly or honestly as their
in-group counterparts.

If you're a team member, here's how to tell if you're in the in-group or the
out-group. And this comes straight from the mouth of a CEO who I have
a lot of respect for. Their take on it was simply: my in-group get their
messages responded to quickly. And in their preferred format. The out-
group have to wait longer, and they might get an email when they prefer
texting, as an example.

Oh, and if you're in the in-group, you'll most likely be provided with
privileges and perks that the out-group isn't. And you'll have more of a voice
during decision making. In-group team members are heard more than out-
group team members.

Again, this is not all bad, because the goal of the out-group team members
should be to get to the in-group. By doing good work, and by becoming a
valued team member. And needless to say, it's incumbent upon leaders to
be self-aware enough to understand who's in their out-group, and work on
developing more trust in those team members. Remember, as much as you
think you're hiding your feelings about in- and out-group team members,
they already know what group they're in.

THREE ROUTINE SHAPING.

The issue with in- and out-groups is that, in LMX theory, in-groups get more in, and out-groups get more out. It's a self-fulfilling prophecy, as team members respond to the way they're treated, and generally respond in kind. For leaders, this is a challenge, as leaders need to be willing to open their mind and increase the trust that they have in the out-group team members. The issue is that the in-group treatment or the out-group treatment becomes routine for the leader. It becomes habitual. And that is scary.

Because habits are heuristics. They are the path of least resistance, and they are hard to break. Breaking bad habits takes effort, and willingness.

If you're a leader reading this, hang onto your hat, because here's something that you can do. It comes under routine shaping (although it is the positive spin on this part of LMX theory).

Leaders—and we train this regularly—need to use a routine to lean into systems leadership. Systems leadership is about creating habits, not being slave to them. It's about using your calendar and your schedule to create systems that hold you accountable to elevate the way you interact with the out-group team members.

Schedule one-on-ones. Schedule career conversations. Schedule walk-around time. Schedule important conversations, so that every one of your team members knows how important they are. In team meetings, schedule time for each team member to contribute. To have a say. To have an input. When it comes to routine shaping, create routines that serve you, not that sabotage you. Schedule it, and then be present.

Then, ask bigger questions. And trust your team members to do their best work. Including providing the growth opportunities for them to do that.

Approach each person with a positive perspective, and elevate your LMX.

WHAT WE CAN LEARN FROM THE BIGGEST PLANT ON EARTH

There's one plant on Earth that doesn't have a stem. It doesn't have any roots, and doesn't have any flowers. It only opens for six whole days, at the end of its 13-month gestation period. It's a plant that we can learn a lot from.

I did a video on this same topic this week, but I felt like I needed to further explain what we can learn from the Rafflesia plant in this section. Why? Because I got to see the Rafflesia plant, in full bloom. Which is extremely lucky, and rare, because of its short blooming period.

It was such an amazing experience that I couldn't stop thinking about it.

Here's what I think the Rafflesia can teach us about perspective.

ONE THIS PLANT STARTS WITH NOTHING.

The Rafflesia plant starts from basically nothing. It's a pod. Thirteen months before it blooms, from nothing, it starts growing. It continues growing, until it's ready to bloom. And bloom it does. It blooms with the biggest leaves on planet Earth. Then, it dies.

It's a truly amazing plant. Amazing to see. I consider it a privilege to have been lucky enough to see it. If you ever need inspiration to achieve something great in your life, think of the Rafflesia plant. It starts with nothing, but becomes the biggest flowering plant on the planet. If you need confidence, start where you are now. Start, even if you're just a pod. Start, even if you don't have enough resources. Even if you don't have everything you think you need.

Just start. And see what you can achieve in the next thirteen months.

TWO DO WHAT IT TAKES.

Question—is thirteen months a long time? It's the whole life of a Rafflesia. The Rafflesia works hard to get ready to bloom. It'll do what it takes to open its massive leaves, which are at least six feet across (in my estimation).

Here's the thing. In the life of a business owner, thirteen months is not really a long time. Or is it? Here's my experience...

I grossly overestimated what I could achieve in twenty years in business. And I grossly underestimated what I could achieve in thirteen months. t\ Thirteen months is over a year. A year. You can achieve so much in a year.

And you know what? I've never gone hard for thirteen months. At least not as hard as I should have. I've never gone as hard as the Rafflesia and committed everything to a cause. Until now. Watch this space.

THREE BE THE BIGGEST AND THE BEST.

This was the amazing thing about the Rafflesia. You have to be lucky to actually see it in bloom. It's the biggest plant on earth, and it has the most vivid flower colour—red, with white spots. Not only does it grow, but it also grows into something everyone wants to see.

And a fun fact is that the Malaysian family that own the land that contains the Rafflesia plants charges an admission fee for every person to go in and see it. For the six days that the plant is in bloom there. They put a sign up out the front, and people stop. People fall over themselves to get to see this plant in bloom. I would have paid twice as much as they charged.

The message is to be the person that everyone else wants to see. The business that everyone else wants to work with. The content creator that people want to read or watch. The person with the contagiously positive perspective that makes big things happen.

Yes, you can become that. In thirteen months.

WHAT I LEARNT FROM WRITING 100 PIECES OF CONTENT THIS YEAR

I used to suck at writing content. I used to suck at being consistent with it. And I used to suck at being confident to put things out there into the content-verse. Because it's hard to do all of those three things for a long period of time.

This year, my focus was on written content, and the team's content strategy has been built around a Wednesday blog and LinkedIn post, and a Friday LinkedIn newsletter. Recently (because we number them in our filing structure), we hit the 100 mark for written content pieces. We might have missed one or two during the year, but in general terms, we were pretty consistent the whole time.

The process is: I write it, the team posts it. A team effort. There were days though (like today—when I'm hungover and writing this at 6 a.m. on December 23), when the absolute last thing I feel like doing is writing a newsletter story. But then I get started, and I get into it because I love the process of putting thoughts on pages.

Here's what the commitment taught me about the importance of keeping a positive perspective.

ONE WITHOUT A SCHEDULE, NOTHING HAPPENS.

This is the biggest thing for me this year, and it works in every area of my life. My calendar is king. I can safely say that if it's not in my calendar, it won't get done. Period.

Every week, on Tuesday, there is a calendar reminder to write content for

Wednesday (and on Wednesday, in case I miss it on Tuesday—double whammy). Same same on Thursday for Friday.

We also have a content calendar, that has all of the content ideas in it. So, with the calendar, combined with the content headings, the writing gets done. The thinking decreases significantly, and there's no such thing as writer's block.

And I know this one isn't that sexy, and it's not ground-breaking, but sometimes things don't need to be earth shattering to be the tip you need to get into and stay in action. There have been many times, when I see that in my calendar not done, and I get it done last minute. It gets done, though.

TWO NOT EVERYONE READS YOUR STUFF.

Not everyone reads your content, and that's OK.

Of the 13k-ish followers that I have on LinkedIn, each of my written pieces gets between about 400 and 1,000 views on average. Earlier in the year, the Friday newsletters were regularly over 1,000 views, but then LinkedIn changed an algorithm, and all of those views instantly halved (even the previous posts halved). Which is cool.

I work with heaps of influencer types, and for them, that's a tragedy. For me, I've always been OK with a little reach, and not a viral reach. Because I write both for readers, and for me. Obviously, I try and put information out into the universe that helps others, but at the same time, I find writing cathartic. I find it something that I can do, to collect my thoughts and ideas. And the content gets repurposed. It's on blogs. On other social media sites. And in my range of books.

The strange part about it is that our business is always growing. And because we don't do any reach-out marketing (we are going to start that soon—I have a business that has never really been marketed), and we keep expanding. When I ask the team what's happening, and what's changing, they always say they think it's because more people are seeing our content.

I'm not sure about that. I feel it's about old-fashioned service, and turning up for our clients each and every time. I haven't missed a client engagement in eighteen years, in sickness or in health. Regardless of what's driving our growth, the one thing I know is that you don't need to go viral to get traction.

THREE YOU MIGHT NEED TO BE CONTROVERSIAL.

If there's one massive lesson that I've learnt this year, this is it. Be controversial, and say what you think.

I've never really been controversial, but I'm confident and comfortable enough now to actually say what I think. I look back over my content, and it's very vanilla. It's nice. It certainly isn't controversial and doesn't talk about the big topics. Not the big ideas, and not the big news. It's positive.

But a positive perspective doesn't necessarily mean writing positive content. Personally, I am now (after all these years) ready to share personal thoughts, beliefs, and opinions. Having a positive perspective helps you to be brave enough to put the ideas out there, because they're worth sharing.

Recently I've been focused on video, more than written content, and that will give me the platform to share more of myself and who I am. Which may get more or less views—who knows what can happen (refer to point two above).

My message to a first-time content creator would be to be real. Don't try to please everyone, don't try to be too professional and too proper. Just say it how it is, and put it out there with the positive intent that it'll do someone good. Don't try to offend people, but if you're controversial, you will say things that aren't popular. Just ask Dr Jordan B Peterson.

ACTIVITY 1.2
DEVELOP A POSITIVE PERSPECTIVE

Take some time now to think about what you've learnt in the last chapter.

Answering the series of questions on the following pages will help you to develop a positive perspective, so you can upgrade your mindset and perform better in your leadership role.

Alternatively, consider journalling. Sitting and writing about your challenges and how you view and deal with them can help to put them all in perspective, so you can move forward more confidently. With a positive perspective, and with a lot less rumination and worry.

What are some things you persist with doing, even though they don't serve you?

What reward or benefit do some of your limiting beliefs give you?

When you're under pressure, what's your primary response (freeze-and-freak-out, fight-and-fend-off, flight-and-!@#k-off, or care and connect)?

If your primary response isn't a good one, can you think of ways you can change to a more adaptive response?

When you fail, what strategies do you use to work through and overcome it? What strategy could work better for you?

In what ways could you be more flexible in accommodating your team members? In what ways could you operate with more care factor?

Can you think of ways you can elevate your LMX (during role taking, role making, and routine shaping)?

What tasks could you schedule to better manage your time?

SKILL III

THINK ABOUT YOUR THOUGHTS

I WONDER IF, BEFORE WE ALL GOT SUCKED INTO THE SCREENS AND THE SOUND BITES, WE SPENT MORE TIME INTROSPECTING.

Thinking about how we feel, and why. Even if it's just spending time in quiet, and spending time with ourselves.

Introspection is a concept (and skill) that is attributed to Wilhelm Wundt, one of the earliest Psychologists, in the late 1800s. Probably when we weren't as busy, and things weren't as stressful.

As a leader, especially under pressure, introspection is a key skill. It allows you to stop, slow down, and focus. Focus on something else, other than the event or the situation that you're coping with in the moment.

The best way to think in an introspective way is to ask yourself questions. And not questions that start with why. Why me? Why now? Why this? Those questions don't help. What and how questions are best, and they'll help you unpack what you feel. What emotions you are experiencing? And how will you channel those emotions for good? And how will you do that in a responsive way, not in a reactive way?

It's amazing how a moment of introspection can bring calm to your day. And calm to the moment.

Introspection, or versions of it, are the first part of emotional intelligence. Emotional intelligence starts with a self-awareness of your emotional state and putting a name to the emotion. Then, it's a matter of regulating the emotion. Fun fact: there are humans who struggle to name the emotion. They struggle to answer the question 'what are you feeling?' The name for that is alexithymia. Alexithymia is a Greek word, attributed to Freud, and it translates as 'no name for emotions'. Alexithymia can be treated, but that takes time and effort. It's a condition that impacts how people relate to others, and it can be detrimental to relationships for the nearly 10% of the population that are suspected to have it.

In short, when we don't take the time to introspect, and to work through our emotional state and responses, we are in fact taking an alexithymia-based approach to life. We're choosing to ignore what makes us human.

But how do you be introspective? If you asked Siddhartha Gautama (aka: Buddha), you would have been told to be quiet. To meditate. To search for Nirvana from within.

If you asked your leadership coach, I'd coach you to ask yourself questions. To be mindful (what you can see, hear, and touch right now in the moment), and to focus on your thoughts and not the situation. And then to focus on others, and how they're feeling in the moment. Then you can respond to the situation accordingly.

One word of warning here is that introspection can become overthinking (or rumination) if you start to beat yourself up for feeling or acting the way you are. These states are not helpful, and will cause you to feel worse about yourself than better. You'll become reactive, not responsive. Most literature around introspection comes with a warning label: over-introspection can be detrimental. It's like water—the body needs it, but it can drown in it, too. This is the yin and the yang of life!

The more you can introspect, the more you can be in emotional control, behavioural control and situational control. Introspecting helps you to create conscious control—the thing that'll help you to lead better when you're under pressure.

But thinking about your thoughts isn't just introspecting. It's also about going meta, and thinking about how you think in the first place.

How To Use Metacognition To Be A Better Leader

In the 2020s, when I mention the word meta, you could be forgiven for thinking about Facebook and Mark Zuckerberg. During the second half of 2021, CEO and major shareholder, Zuckerberg, announced the name change, to position the former Facebook as a platform that would be part of the metaverse. Aka, 'a composite universe melding online, virtual, and augmented worlds that people can seamlessly traverse' (Credit: New York Times). In short, meta means the next level up.

Instead of thinking Facebook when you think about meta, think studies. If you spend your time (which I am guessing most of you don't) reading research reports and studies, to try and understand what's going on in the world, you'll know there are meta studies. Meta studies are a study of the studies. Researchers will review any number of studies on the same topic and look for similar correlations or causation in the data. That review, and the consequent detail that it produces, is called a meta-study (generally speaking). It's a study of the studies. The next level up.

So, what is metacognition? As a concept, metacognition has been around since 1976 when the term was coined by the American Psychologist John H Flavell. Flavell was interested in the development of children, and he critically analysed the works of the early developmental psychologists like Jean Piaget. Flavell was most intrigued by the theory of mind, which is the ability for children to understand that there are other people in the world that also have feelings and thoughts, just like they do (but different thoughts and feelings to them). This work gave Flavell the insight into how we learn, and how we perform cognitively as adults. And more specifically, how we apply what we've learnt, through cognitive regulation. Metacognition has therefore been described as 'thinking about thinking.' The next level up.

It's probably more specific than that, though. Metacognition is about how you learn and gain knowledge, and then how you apply that knowledge (and if the learning process has been effective).

So, how can leaders use metacognition to think about their thoughts, to influence them, and to take their leadership to the next level?

ONE KNOWLEDGE AS AN ELEMENT OF METACOGNITION.

A lot of the metacognition research work has been focused on students, and classroom settings. Given that leading is about learning though, it's important for leaders to understand how they learn new skills and knowledge. One great report on metacognition that I came across was penned by Emily Lai,[8] who explained that metacognitive knowledge is the knowledge that you have about your cognitive strengths, as well as your cognitive limitations. In other words, what you learn easily and what you don't learn easily. There are three types of metacognitive knowledge: declarative knowledge, procedural knowledge, and conditional knowledge.

Declarative knowledge is what you know about yourself as a learner. What things you learn and remember well, and what things are harder to learn and remember. Like names, or phone numbers, as an example. Or processes, or procedures. Or general knowledge. Or historical dates. A superpower for leaders is to be able to remember things quickly. Understanding how to improve their declarative knowledge will help the leader be better at cognitive processing and information recall. Declarative knowledge is easy to verbalise.

As a leader, how do you learn best? Is it reading, studying, writing, asking questions, listening to an audiobook, watching TED talks, doing classroom training, or something else? And what makes it easier for you

to learn something new?

Procedural knowledge is about having a cognitive understanding of what you do. Procedural knowledge relates to things like riding a pushbike (as a simple example). Which, if you were asked to explain how to do it, would be difficult to verbalise. You just do it. Metacognition challenges you to think about how you do what you do. And what techniques you apply. To think about what rules of thumb (heuristics), or what methods, you apply to your leadership or to certain situations or circumstances. Imagine for a moment trying to explain to someone how you do leadership.

As a leader, how do you do what you do (and why), and how would you explain your thought processes to someone you were coaching?

Conditional knowledge is simply knowledge relating to when, and how, to apply declarative and procedural knowledge to learning. It allows leaders to allocate their cognitive resources to the learning process in a way that makes them more effective at learning (and listening). This is a key element of metacognition, as self-aware leaders know what conditions (internal and external) they learn best in and retain most from.

As a leader, how, when, where, and what do you need to learn to be more effective in your role?

TWO REGULATION AS AN ELEMENT OF METACOGNITION.

The regulation of thinking and learning is about planning what you're going to do, monitoring if you've been effective, and evaluating if you've achieved your overall goals.

Planning is about the identification and selection of the appropriate strategy for the situation or condition. And planning how to learn or work 'in a strategic manner, to achieve a goal or objective' (Credit: Jennifer Livingston).[10] In other words, in a difficult situation, your planning process (and metacognition) will kick in, and you will think through to determine what the best strategy is to apply and what will work best in a situation. And then you can apply the strategy to your learning or your situation.

Planning: As a leader, what strategies do you have available to you, for when you're under stress or duress (internal or external pressure)? You can do some of that thinking in advance!

Deep reflection (after the event) or introspection (during the event, in the moment) is the key leadership and metacognitive skill—and one that should be practiced as much and as regularly as possible. Reflection is a learnt skill, and it's like keeping a mental (or written) journal of your experiences, and why you will or won't take the same approach into the future.

Monitoring: If you do nothing else after reading this section, please think about how you can add reflection to your leadership and life. And you might think you're doing it well already, and that's great. Make sure that it is reflection, though, and not rumination (big difference: one is positive, and one isn't).

Evaluation is about reflection and looking back on the situation with a critical eye and determining if you made the right decision and if you applied the right strategy. This is about asking metacognitive questions, like 'how well did I do'?, and 'what would I do differently next time?' It's the first and most basic part of reflection, but it's more of a high-level review of your outcome. It's somewhat binary, and is about a yes or a no.

Evaluation: As a leader, think about a situation that you've been through, where you've tried to learn something, or you've had to solve a problem. Unpack what went well and what didn't.

That's metacognition, in a nutshell. It's not complex, and it's completely worth the effort to understand and apply it—because thinking about your thoughts is one of the most effective ways to move them into line with what you want to achieve, and who you want to be as a leader.

HOW TO BE A CONSCIOUS LEADER, AND WHY

Thinking about your thoughts is one of the best ways to become a conscious leader—which is a good leader.

As a leader coach, I regularly hear the words 'old-school leader' and 'new-age leader'. I coach a mix of both types of leaders, and if I was to describe the difference between the two, it would be that new-age leaders are more connected to other humans. They're more transformational in their approach. And more importantly, they're more emotionally competent. These leaders take a real 'people' approach to leadership.

Old-school leaders tend to be more transactional in their approach. They're more direct, and they tend to be too busy for all that touchy-feely stuff, like dealing with feelings. These leaders are typically more interested in production than people. They can't understand why people can't just chip in and get the work done.

And it's not up to me to tell leaders that they should be one way or the other. My job is to help leaders create psychologically safe and high-performing teams, whatever that process looks like for each individual. It's different for everyone. The one strategy I share with leaders who want to be more new age is to lean into being a conscious leader. Now, for some, this is a big shift, but worth the effort! And it's well explained in the book of the same name, by John Mackey, Steve McIntosh, and Carter Phipps.[12]

Be ready for a shift in mindset, though, as this is a leadership style that uses big words like 'love' and 'care factor' and 'virtues' and 'connection.'

One comment in the book relates to one reader's take on conscious leadership, and they noted that:

> **Rarely does a book move me to tears, yet this one did, by holding up a mirror to the kind of leader I most deeply want to be. Conscious leadership is a powerful invitation to shift our mindset from the win/lose games of war to the community-building virtues of love, authenticity, and integrity. It's a book built on the radical idea that business can be a force for bringing more love into the world. Count me in.**

And:

> **Leaders today are called to a faster pace, sharper strategy, and broader responsibilities, but also to greater awareness, humility, and authenticity. Conscious Leadership will help you summon the courage to open your heart, dig deeper, and keep growing as a conscious leader.**

There are three elements of conscious leadership, which both influence your thoughts, and are the product of them. They include:

ONE VISION AND VIRTUE.

Vision and virtue are about having a strong direction and sharing that with your team in a way that they can connect with it. The vision is about purpose, and the virtue piece is about behaviour (the word virtue is defined as behaviour that's based on a high moral compass).

Vision and virtue are broken down into purpose first, lead with love, and always act with integrity. Putting purpose first means doing the work to make sure that your team is clear on their purpose, and that it aligns with your purpose as the leader. And it's about having a bigger purpose, and one that's worth working for.

Leading with love is about putting people first and knowing that humanity is the key concern when it comes to leadership. There's a ripple effect caused by leaders, where leaders' actions ripple out through the team member, to their families, and to society. Leaders have the rare ability to impact a wide range of people through their leadership and love.

Acting with integrity is about doing what's right, and doing what you say you're going to do. Integrity is perhaps the most respected value in leaders, and leaders that fall out of credibility with their teams generally lack integrity.

LEADER ACTION

Challenge yourself to do a self-assessment on how strongly you lead with vision and virtue, and ask yourself if you put love and people first.

TWO MINDSET AND STRATEGY.

Mindset and strategy relate to thinking differently about business. Not doing business to win, but doing business to make a difference. Not treating business as a war to be waged, but as a value to be added. Not as a short-term pursuit, but as an infinite game (Simon Sinek-esque)[18] of building long-term relationships. Then, with a mindset like that, putting strategies in place to deliver on the long-term goal of doing leadership to grow businesses and to grow people to add long-term value.

Mindset and strategy are broken down specifically into finding win-win-win solutions, innovating, creating value, and thinking long term. Conscious leadership is about having a positive-sum world view. As Alexander McCobin, CEO of Conscious Capitalism, puts it, 'A positive-sum worldview is a foundational premise of capitalism, where we seek out mutually beneficial exchanges so that we create more value for everyone than existed before the exchange.'

Having a win-win-win approach highlights that there is an onus on leaders to think about the team, the business, and the society in which we all live and operate.

LEADER ACTION

Think about your leadership strategy for a moment, and about how what you do could have a bigger impact on your team and on society. And if you're in business, how your actions are helping others win, too.

THREE PEOPLE AND CULTURE.

People and culture should be the focus for all leaders. All great leaders are supported by great teams, and those great teams don't get great by accident. The leaders of great (high-performing) teams understand how important culture is, and how important it is to have a growth mindset. The growth of team members is a key driver for conscious leaders.

People and culture are further broken down into constantly evolving the team, regularly revitalising, and continuously learning and growing. For me, this is the cornerstone of leadership, and conscious leaders take people and culture to the next level. By fostering a culture of learning and coaching. By making personal and professional growth a priority. Not just talking about it, but ensuring that team members are challenged to develop their technical and relationship skills.

As part of this section, there is a cool take on revitalisation that I love from the book that talks about leaders being able to unplug and power down, and supporting their teams to do the same.

> **For leaders in any field or area of expertise, the power of rest, repose, relaxation, and rejuvenation should never be underestimated. It might seem counterintuitive to suggest that such passive, quiescent activities can be the fount of dynamism and creativity, but that's exactly the point. Indeed, there may be few things that spur productivity more than those behaviours that allow us to empty our mind of prosaic mental clutter.**

LEADER ACTION

Take some time out of your busy schedule to recharge your batteries and help your team to do the same.

As you reflect on the above, think about your thoughts, and how bringing them into line them with the strategies of conscious leadership could help you and your team to grow and develop into a high-performing team.

THE SUBTLE ART OF THINKING FAST AND TALKING SLOW

Most people struggle to think on their feet. Especially leaders. More especially, leaders under pressure. And that's the most important time to be able to practice the fine art of thinking fast and talking slow. But what does that really mean?

Well, it means multitasking your emotionality and your languaging. And this is the only thing on planet Earth that can effectively be classed as multi-tasking (according to Anton Guinea, of The Guinea Group). Most psychology texts will tell you that multitasking isn't a thing; it's called task switching. I'm here to tell you that if you can't multitask what's in your heart and head with what comes out of your mouth, you'll struggle to connect with other hominins. Let me explain.

Just reflect for a moment and think about the best communicators that you know. I'm guessing these people don't talk continuously. My theory is that they do very specific things to engage others in dialogue. Their influence is created by doing things like reading the play, listening to understand, and speaking with leader languaging.

Reading the play is about being able to focus on the person you're speaking to, and understanding what's going on for them, while you're having the conversation with them. Good leaders know what the other person's body is doing. Even where their eyes are going (left means they're recalling, and right means they're constructing—Google NLP Eye Patterns, Images, for more information). Reading the play is about being empathetic and feeling what the other person is feeling while you're conversing. Then, tailoring your communication accordingly.

Listening to understand is perhaps the most important of the thinking fast and talking slow skills. When you're listening to understand, you're present. You're caring enough to make the other person your priority in the moment. Regardless of all the stress or pressure that's going on around you. And if you don't understand, ask more questions. Or ask better questions. Don't comment or make a statement until you're clear on what's being communicated to you. Listen more than you speak (use your ears and mouth in the ratio of how many of them you have—2:1) and let silence do the heavy lifting if you need to. You don't have to fill the gap of quiet with words (most people think you do).

Leader languaging is a key skill. Most people don't choose their words carefully. They don't realise that words have power, and talk straight to the limbic system of the brain—the emotional part. Words can be triggers and can change someone's day. Or life. And if you think this is an exaggeration, think back to the time you were most hurt by someone. You'll remember exactly what they said...even if it was thirty years ago. Leaders who can think fast and talk slow have a strong understanding of the power of language, and they choose their words carefully. They choose words that convey the message, but that do no harm.

In summary, the subtle art of thinking fast and talking slow is about helping you build better relationships, build better communication skills, and build better teams. FYI, this is the skill that the great orators and public speakers use. They can focus on the experience that their audience is having, while tailoring their message accordingly.

Yes, it sounds like hard work. But I can tell you, after practicing these skills for the last twenty years of thinking about thoughts, and learning how to change them to be a better leader, it's worth the effort!

MANAGING YOUR TIME AND CARING FOR YOUR TEAM AT THE SAME TIME

Your thoughts underpin how you behave as a leader. And thinking about how to bring them into line with who you want to be as a leader is a critical step in becoming that leader. But it's hard, when you're under pressure.

The modern leader arrives at the office. They're greeted with a new and long list of unread emails and cannot possibly understand how they all came in overnight. Before they sit down, their phone is starting to buzz with messages and requests for their time. Then the phone rings with another catastrophe to attend to. Or so it seems.

They think that today might be the day that they finally lose their self-control. And they know that they aren't behaving in a way that a great leader would. How can they? They're nervous, worried, anxious…they're under pressure. And there's no letting up.

And then one of their team members knocks on the door, and needs their support, and their undivided attention. Just think about what their teams must be going through if the leader is under so much pressure.

How can leaders take a step back, and pull themselves out of the stress and pressure that they find themselves in? And how can they influence their thinking to bring it into line with good working leadership that gives team members the care and attention that they need?

Here are three hot tips.

ONE BE STILL, BREATHE, AND BE IN CONTROL.

This really is easier said than done, though making the effort is certainly worth it. In resilience speak, this part is called getting composed, and being present. As much as you have a heap of other things to deal with, being still and breathing are the most important things you can do to be present for everyone in your team.

They need you in control. Team members can tell when you're not. We've surveyed team members, and asked them what they want from their leaders, and the responses are care factor and consistency. Consistency of emotional state. Not a roller coaster. Yes, staying in control is a skill. Yes, you can get in control just by breathing into your stomach and oxygenating your brain's frontal lobes. Your team will appreciate it.

TWO BE OPEN, AND STEP INTO CARE FACTOR.

Be open with your body language, and open with your head and heart. Stepping into care factor is about listening to your team, and their challenges, and giving them the support they need in the moment (their issues are major for them right now). Mistake number one that leaders make is to be tapping away on a keyboard when team members are talking, sharing ideas, or asking for support.

And you won't believe this—I've been asked in the past to coach a leader on how to be more ignorant, so that team members can see they're working and stop bothering them. True story (but I didn't, of course). Stepping into care factor is stepping into psychological safety, where leaders are listeners.

THREE BE COURAGEOUS, AND GIVE AWAY SOME RESPONSIBILITY.

This is the process stuff. Be clear on the priority of the issue. Be clear on whose issue it is. Be clear on the solutions. If there are none offered, prompt for them. Be clear on actions moving forward. Decide to support, where you can, and task allocate regardless. Maybe you don't need to take it all on yourself, and you can get the monkey off your back. You can own the issue without owning the action. You can change your thoughts, which can change your actions.

After all that's done, at about 8:10 a.m., or whatever time you've started for the day, go to the coffee machine.

ANTON, I'M NOT A NARCISSIST, AM I?

I got asked that very question in a leadership coaching session recently. By a leader who'd been told that they were a narcissist.

Which isn't that uncommon these days, as more and more leaders (and their teams) learn about psychology, and what drives behaviour. Narcissism is like the buzz word of right now. And, at times, rightly so. Thinking about your thoughts can reveal the ones that are working for you and your team—and the ones that aren't.

Here's how I answered the question—and if you know me well enough, you'll know it was with some questions of my own. Here are the three questions I asked (note that I have taken some poetic license to tell the story in a way that makes sense and talks to the topic of narcissism).

Question: Do you know what narcissism is?
Answer: Well, yeah, sort of? Making it all about me, right? Or being aggressive, maybe.
Discussion: Ish.

There are generally three types of narcissism (and these are all explained differently, depending on the text that you read). Let's look at it, not from a psych perspective, which would talk about it as a diagnosable personality disorder, but from a leadership perspective. The three types of narcissism include exhibitionist, closet, and toxic narcissism.

Exhibitionist narcissists (also called grandiose narcissists) take a 'look at me' approach to life. It's all about them. They want to be in the spotlight, and they think they're better than everyone else. 'They think they're amazing— they think themselves to be smarter, better-looking, more powerful than other people, and they pretty much believe it' (Credit: Business Insider). In short, they're over-confident, and they really don't care what others think about them.

As a leader, they're always right. They're doing the best job. They can't be told. And they certainly don't think your idea is better than theirs.

Closet narcissists (also called vulnerable narcissists) take a 'poor me' approach to life. It's all about them, but they play the victim card. It's the behaviour of these narcissists that created the term 'gaslighting' which is about always feeling bad about yourself when you're around a closet narcissist. They're passive aggressive, and nothing is their fault. They want to be grandiose, but don't know how. And they're frustrated by that. They're chameleons and are nice to you one minute (maybe in public) and not so much the next (maybe in private).

As a leader, they're unpredictable. Their team members will never feel good about themselves, but they won't know why. Their team members don't ever feel worthy or valued. Or cared for.

Toxic narcissists (also called chaotic narcissists) take a 'wilful damage' approach to life. They thrive on (and actively cause) chaotic situations. This is the worst type of narcissist, as they go out of their way to be destructive and malevolent. Toxic narcissists 'are perfectly fine destroying the careers of other people, basically fine with just imploding people emotionally, physically, and spiritually' (Credit: Business Insider). It's safe to say that you don't want to be in the team of a toxic narcissist.

As a leader, they are very, very harmful. Their team members not only feel hurt, but they're really hurt. Their careers are damaged. Their emotions are damaged. Their resilience is damaged. And all very overtly. Out in public, for all to see.

It's worth noting that narcissism is characterised (generally) by grandiose behaviour and fantasies, arrogance and entitlement, very low levels of empathy, and a need for admiration and attention.

Question: Why did the person think you're a narcissist?
Answer: I'm actually not sure. I didn't ask, I was really taken aback by the conversation, and it hurt a bit to be called that. I've never been called that before. Though there are times when I could have acted like all three of those types.
Discussion: Great. An honest response. And narcissism is considered by some as a spectrum. That is, we're all on the spectrum, and tend to be narcissistic, even if it's only in a very small way.

Here's the big thing, and this is what we work through in our leadership programs. Do you feel like you're helping more than you're hindering? Do you feel like you're healing more than you're harming? What I mean by that is that leadership, by definition, is about lifting people up, not putting them down. It's about being a good human, and leaving people better than you found them, even when you must have robust conversations.

Leadership interactions should be done in a positive and empathetic way, that does no harm. Here are the big three questions to ask yourself, if you feel like you could be considered narcissistic:

- Is my intent good, or is it to harm others? (You need to answer this honestly—a true narcissist doesn't have the right intent.)

- Am I aggressive, abusive, or abrupt in my delivery or interactions? (If so, that's uncool too—because it means that you're happy to keep hurting others.)

- Can I be empathetic, and understand what others are experiencing? (If not, that's very uncool—because it means that you're not only happy to hurt others, but also that you have zero understanding of the impact that both your behaviour and the experiences of others has on their emotional state.)

Question: Where to from here?
Answer: I think we can always continue to do self-development work. So, I'm going to take it on as a challenge to work on how I show up as a leader. If you were me, what would you recommend?

Discussion: Great question. Here are the things that you could consider as an action plan to continue your leadership development. And maybe don't think about this as an 'anti-narcissism' plan; think about it as a 'working on being an even better leader' plan.

- **It's not about you!** Remember that leadership is about the team performance, and the individuals in the team, and their development. The easiest way to be a great leader is to be thinking about how you can support your team to become a better version of itself, and to take your team to higher levels of performance. Where your focus goes, your energy flows—if you think about your team, you'll be more likely to be seen as a caring and connected leader.

- **Empathy can be learnt.** Remember that being able to empathise with other humans is potentially the most important skill you can learn as a leader. And yes, it can be learnt. If you're up for it. Empathy is about being able to think through (cognition) what it might be like for the other person in this situation. Then, feeling (emotions) what it is that they might be feeling. The big part of empathy is compassion (action). Every single human is born compassionate. But it can take effort at times to go out of your way to help another human when they're in need. It is worth it, though.

- **Create conscious control.** This is the big one! Without conscious control (emotional, situational, and behavioural control), you'll never maintain great relationships with your team members. Thinking fast and talking slow is the key skill required to manage your emotions. Which is basically about knowing what your triggers are, and responding, not reacting, to situations, circumstances, or human behaviour. And doing no harm.

Thinking about your thoughts can help you to identify patterns in your thinking that are helping others—and the ones that are hurting them. It's a critical step in changing your thinking to steady yourself on your path to becoming a leader who works with purpose to reach their 'why'.

SIMON SINEK IS ONTO SOMETHING WITH FINDING YOUR 'WHY'

But what is your 'why'? Thinking about how you think will tell you.

Leaders who are part of our coaching or training programs get to work through why they do leadership. My observations are that at least 90% of the leaders we work with haven't done the exercise of clarifying why they lead other humans.

As a leader, your team doesn't buy into what you do or how you do it. They buy into why you do it (thanks Simon Sinek).[18] But if you don't know why you do leadership, how can you share that with others?

It's such an important concept—let's unpack why.

FIRSTLY, THOUGH...

If it's so important understand your why, what's the reason that so many leaders have never thought about it? When I ask leaders why they do leadership, the three most common answer are: 1) Because I was on the spot, and no-one else wanted to fill in; 2) Because I was a good technician; and 3) Because it pays more. And I get it, these three are the main reasons that people end up leading other humans. Cool.

But when you're there, surely the importance of the role kicks in, given that, after parenting, leadership is the second most important role on planet Earth? Surely leaders sit back and think about why they put themselves through the daily hustle of leading?

Apparently, they don't very often. Maybe it's a business thing, or maybe they just never get around to it.

NOT THAT QUICKLY ...

I won't let you off that easily. Sorry in advance. No excuses. Accountability. Take the time, make the effort, and put the thinking into why leadership is your calling (if it is). Then share that with your team. And let it drive your behaviour, and influence theirs.

IT REALLY DOES MAKE A DIFFERENCE

And if you do the exercise properly, you'll be amazed at how much value you get from it. We have hundreds of examples of leaders going from wide eyed to confident in sharing their why. The secret is simple, and thanks again, Simon Sinek.[18]

Grab a pen and paper. Think about your leadership. Start with the two words 'I believe.' Then keep writing. Finish the sentence at least three times, and then not only write it, but feel it. Feel just how important those beliefs (and values) are to you. And when you know that your beliefs drive your behaviour, you can be true to yourself when you're leading. By giving limiting beliefs away, drawing from positive beliefs, and stepping into your why.

This really is a powerful process. Check out Simon Sinek's work for more information on how to do it.

How To Have A Real Conversation With Your Leadership Coach

Recently, I got an email from a coaching client, who expressed how grateful they were that we had had 'a real conversation.' It was my first session with this client, and it was great feedback to get after just one session.

Of course, I asked what they thought made it a real conversation, and the answer was around the topics that we covered. We talked through big issues like their inferiority complex, imposter syndrome, fear of failure, and a range of other topics that most people aren't comfortable to discuss. The heavy stuff, the real stuff! It works, because they're thinking about their thoughts, and figuring out how to change them.

What I shared is that coaching sessions work best when our clients are willing to open up their hearts, and really unpack what's happening for them. What their fears are. What their frustrations are, and what they're focused on right now.

Let's look at these separately.

ONE WHAT ARE YOUR REAL FEARS?

What things are you putting off because you're scared to confront them? Most of the time, this is a conversation, or a range of conversations, that our clients are avoiding. Fear (false expectations appearing real) stops us from taking action. It means that we overthink what could go wrong, instead of focusing on what could go right.

Public speeches or job interviews are the two main things that people bring to sessions for support with. These situations can cause a range of emotions for people, and they can cause our clients a great deal of stress—until we talk through them and work out how they should approach the situation. Usually with heaps of preparation, is the coaching advice I provide.

LEADER ACTION

Yes, some conversations are very difficult to have, and some could even be relationship enders. But most don't end up nearly as bad as you imagine they will. The sooner your deal with worry and anxiety, the sooner you find the confidence to get through the situation, and the better you'll feel!

TWO WHAT ARE YOUR FRUSTRATIONS?

This is the area that we spend most time talking about. Rightly so. Leaders are under pressure. They're stressed, and they're crazy busy. They get frustrated by a range of things, including not getting enough support from their leaders or their teams. Not being able to resolve a dispute. Or not being able to move forward on a project. Among a myriad of other things.

Leading under pressure falls right into that category. Recently, I was discussing this point with a client, and learned that one of the key leadership skills for managing frustration is consistency: of emotional response, and of temperament. In other words, creating conscious control.

LEADER ACTION

Yes, leadership is stressful. There are things that cause frustration. So, it's important to deal with frustrations. And it's important not to over-share with your teams just how frustrated you are. That's your challenge to deal with as a leader.

THREE WHAT'S YOUR FOCUS, RIGHT NOW?

Probably my favourite part of coaching sessions. When a client comes to me and says, 'right, I need a hand to develop this, or build that, or create this.' Great, let's get the presentation built, or the business case mapped out. Or the process developed.

This is good, fun work. I've worked with clients on everything from position descriptions, to five-year plans, and everything in between, giving the leader a different perspective. Fun fact: I was working with a leader on a restructure during one session of two hours, that went for six hours.

LEADER ACTION

Yes, there's always something to do, and yes, sometimes a different perspective is useful. Someone outside the organisation and outside of your team can give good ideas and opinions that you may not have considered yet.

In summary, the next time you're sitting down with your leadership coach (reach out if you'd like to become a client of ours), remember to come prepared with your fears, your frustrations, and your current focus areas.

Then, we can have a real conversation.

ACTIVITY 1.3
THINK ABOUT YOUR THOUGHTS

Take some time now to think about what you've learnt in the last chapter.

The following questions will help you to think about your thoughts, develop a better understanding of how you perform in your leadership role and why, and how to improve your conscious control to be a better leader.

As a leader, how do you learn best? Is it reading, studying, writing, asking questions, listening to an audiobook, classroom training, or something else?

As a leader, how, when, where, and what do you need to learn to be more effective in your role?

How would you explain your thought processes to someone you were coaching?

As a leader, how do you lead with vision and virtue?

What are some ways you could do business not to win, but to make a difference?

What are some ways you could be more courageous, and hand over some responsibility to your team?

Do you believe empathy can be learnt? Can you think of ways to further develop your empathy as a leader?

SKILL IV

LEAD UNDER

PRESSURE

SOME LEADERS JUST SEEM TO HAVE IT ALL TOGETHER.

No matter what happens, they stay calm, they don't react (or appear to), they don't fly off the handle, and they seem to just 'take it in their stride.'

All leaders face pressure. Whether the pressure is about the achievement of budgets or numbers, or if it's about always having the solution and being right. Or the pressure that comes from having to make big decisions. Or even having to engage in robust conversations.

Regardless of where the pressure comes from, there are some fundamental 'laws of leadership' that, when applied, will change the life of the leader and make life easier for their team members.

While there are so many skills you need to develop to upgrade your mindset and your leadership, there are a few key skills that you need to learn in order to be a better leader when you're under pressure. The real skills required to lead under pressure include intrapersonal skills, people skills, and information skills. Without them, the pressure will win.

Let's unpack these separately.

ONE INTRAPERSONAL SKILLS.

A long time ago, in a place far, far away, it was thought that your Intelligence Quotient (IQ) was 80% responsible for the success that you'd achieve during your working life. Actually, the place wasn't that far away, and it wasn't that long ago that this belief existed. With the advent of the IQ in the early 1900s, came what researchers thought was the ability to measure how smart people are. And of course, that must determine how successful they would be, right? Not so much.

If it's not IQ, what is responsible for our success, especially as leaders? It must be EQ (Emotional Intelligence) then...and if EQ is more important than IQ, maybe our success is based on something like 80% EQ and 20% IQ. Cotrus, Stanciu and Bulborea (2012)[5] conducted a study on students, to clarify if their success really was dependent in eight parts out of ten on their intelligence quotient, or their emotional intelligence. They confirmed that for students, that was the case.

But many years before that, in 1995, the person responsible for creating the concept of Emotional Intelligence, Daniel Goleman[7], stated very clearly that he didn't think it was possible to come up with what percentage of your success can be attributed to your emotional intelligence. What he did point out though, was that:

> **Emotional intelligence trumps IQ primarily in those 'soft' domains where intellect is relatively less relevant for success—where, for example, emotional self-regulation and empathy may be more salient skills than purely cognitive abilities.**

That is, in the domain of leadership.

In other words, EQ is more important than IQ when people and their emotions are involved. Aka: Leadership.

The intrapersonal skills are those skills that have to be practiced internally, and that need to connect the limbic system of the brain (emotions) to the smart brain (pre-frontal cortex) in order to create control. Emotional control, behavioural control, and situational control. Emotional control is the basis of emotional intelligence.

And, like all intrapersonal skills, the focus of emotional control is around responding not reacting to stimuli. It's about reflecting and rendering. And it's about being present. These skills are simple, but not easy, especially when you're in a BOOM moment or a BOOM period.

The process of emotional control involves emotional self-awareness, then emotional self-regulation. It then involves emotional social-awareness, then emotional social-regulation (in others). A learnt skill set.

If you do nothing else after reading this, just ask yourself, what emotion am I feeling right now, and why?

TWO INTERPERSONAL SKILLS.

The purists might say that emotional intelligence (as discussed above) is actually an interpersonal skill, not an intrapersonal skill, as it's about how we deal with others. I don't concur with this viewpoint, as interpersonal skills are more than emotional intelligence. They include care factor, connection, and character. These skills align with John C. Maxwell's irrefutable Law of Leadership (Law 3) which is the Law of Solid Ground.[13] Leaders who can care, who can connect, and who are strong of character, can engender respect and trust in their team.

When it comes time to lead under pressure, teams must trust their leader. Period. What can happen is that leaders can forget that their teams are feeling the pressure as much as they are. Team members feel the pressure too. But they don't have the information that the leader has, and so are left to make assumptions or presumptions about what's happening.

With some care factor, a level of psychological safety can be achieved, where everyone feels safe to ask questions about the situation or circumstances. Physical safety is a big deal, and keeping people safe during a BOOM event is critical, as is connecting with people on a personal level in order to understand their situation.

Care factor, connection and character can all be demonstrated through empathetic behaviour. Empathy is a key skill of leaders, and one that's being talked about more and more in recent times. But what is it? It's the ability to put ourselves in others' shoes, and understand their position, and their emotional state. For sure. But real empathy (again unpacked by Daniel Goleman[7]) is about compassion.

Compassion is taking action. Compassion is not a feeling. It's taking action to make someone's life better. In psychology, we know that the vast majority of humans (like bonobo monkeys, our closest relatives) are born compassionate. That is, we're wired to care for and help others. Cortes, Barragan, Brooks, and Meltzof (2012)[4] studied at what age children would give up food, even when they were hungry, to help another child. Nineteen months was the age that children would voluntarily share their food— sharing without being told they had to.

So why, when the BOOM moments happen, do we become less compassionate? Why, in the moments when others need us the most, do we focus on ourselves, to the detriment of our teams?

If you do nothing else after reading this, go and see what you can do to help out a team member or even a perfect stranger.

THREE INFORMATIONAL SKILLS.

The informational skills, or process skills, are those skills that are about using information to make decisions. Leaders need courage to 'make decisions under fire.' Yes, there is fear, but yes, there needs to be action. That action includes making decisions, delegating, and disseminating information, no matter the pressure.

Obtaining the right information in the first place is as important as what you do with it. A bad decision made with correct information is much better than a bad decision made with little or wrong information.

The process is face fears, make decisions, and have a future focus. The future focus ensures that the leader is looking to the longer term, as well as fighting the current BOOM fire.

And delegate. This word is somewhat overused in leadership circles, and can sometimes nearly be touted as the panacea for all leadership woes. That's not the case, but what is certain is that when the pressure is on, the more people that are responding to the BOOM event in a controlled way, the better the outcome.

Leading under pressure means not taking on everything yourself. It means drawing on others for support—which helps you, and empowers them.

HOW TO EMPOWER OTHERS LIKE LARRY PAGE

Lawrence Edward Page was born on 26 March 1973, in Lansing, Michigan, USA. Larry Page had an unusual beginning. His parents were both professors in the field of computing. Dr. Carl Victor Page, Larry's father, taught at Michigan State University as a professor of computer science and artificial intelligence. Gloria Page, Larry's mother, taught computer programming. This might not be remarkable now, but in the early 1970s, computers were a new science, not even grasped by the general public. Larry Page's future might have been set before he was born.

The house where Page grew up was full of early computers and copies of *Popular Science* magazines. This strange environment allowed Page to begin tinkering with computers when he was a child, which is exactly what he did, for the rest of his life.

Following his school years, he studied Computer Engineering at the University of Michigan, before enrolling in graduate studies at Stanford University. Page had begun working on a project related to the World Wide

Web, encouraged by a professor. Page was looking at the ways in which web pages were linked to one another. At first, Page worked on a way to find out how many pages on the web were linked to any other page. Search engines at that time could only determine how many times any particular word appeared on a certain page. Therefore, web searches produced results simply based on particular words and often returned huge lists of irrelevant searches.

Page was interested in ranking pages, or websites, based not purely on the frequency of a word, but also on the number of links that led from a site to any given other site. His friend Sergey Brin had expertise in data mining, having already written over a dozen papers on the subject. Brin was interested because of the project's complexity. At that time, there were an estimated 10 million pages on the web, any of which could potentially be linked to any other. The two went to work on the complex project, and the result was two papers.

The second paper, with the mouthful of a title, The Anatomy of a Large-Scale Hypertextual Web Search Engine[1], made a splash in tech circles. Soon after they wrote it, the paper had been downloaded more frequently than almost any other scientific document on the internet. They had developed their new search engine, describing it in that paper. The program was then called 'BackRub', and it was run on the motley collection of personal computers in Page's dormitory room.

Very quickly, the two boys realised that they were onto something. They renamed the page, and the google.com domain name was registered in 1997. The name was chosen as a derivation of the word 'googol', which is the name of an enormous number that consists of a one followed by 100 zeros. They chose the name to represent the enormous amounts of data that would be coordinated by their search engine.

Fast forward to 2010, when two co-authors and myself released an international best-selling book (Millionaires and Billionaires—Secrets Revealed), which included a chapter on Larry Page, and Google employed around 24,400 staff. It now employs over 156,000 staff. Page doesn't simply think in terms of providing a quality service to make Google the best search engine. He thinks big, and puts that thinking into his business. In everything Page and Google do, he has an eye towards improving the world. He set up his company that way: he makes sure that his employees are empowered to work in that way, and he wants to offer users the tools to work that way, too. He says, 'talented people are attracted to Google because we empower them to change the world.'

The above paragraphs are an excerpt from the chapter on Larry Page, but I'm fascinated by one word that Page uses, and that is to 'empower' talented people. So, what does that really mean? Some people that I've asked about empowerment call it enabling, or trusting, or some other derivative of being authorised to make a change, or to make a difference.

So, how can you empower others, even when you're leading under pressure, and how can you do it like Larry Page and Google?

To answer this question, let's first understand what empowerment is. And let's turn to the organisational psychology definition, which is psychological empowerment. Psychological empowerment is defined as an 'intrinsic task motivation reflecting a sense of self-control in relation to one's work and an active engagement with one's work role' (Meng and Sun, 2019).[16]

There are four key concepts of psychological empowerment, which include Meaning, Impact, Competence, and Self-determination.

ONE MEANING.

Meaning is about how much a person's work helps them achieve their personal goals and objectives. It's about how much their work lines up with their self-identity. How much their work is aligned with their personal values, and how much their work can help them express themselves. Meaning is the most personal element of the work experience. It's also perhaps the most important.

TWO IMPACT.

Impact is different to meaning, in that it's how a person's work helps them contribute to their organisation's goals and objectives. And how much their work adds value to something bigger than themself. This is about value proposition, and being involved in work that makes a difference to the output of an organisation.

THREE COMPETENCE.

Competence is simply how able staff feel to do their jobs and perform the functions required of them. Feeling competent is related to feeling confident and capable, and it's developed from skills, knowledge, and experience. People who feel competent feel like they can deal with the demands of their role, and they aren't easily overwhelmed.

FOUR SELF-DETERMINATION.

Self-determination means having a high level of input into how a person performs in their role. It's about a level of autonomy that suits the team member, and that suits the organisation. Having self-determination means having a say in your position description, and your work in general. And it's about having a level of control over your destiny.

Team members who feel like they're high in the four areas of psychological empowerment will say things like 'My work activities are personally meaningful to me' (meaning); 'I have significant influence over what happens in my department' (impact); 'I'm confident about my ability to do my job' (competence); and 'I have significant autonomy in determining how I do my job' (self-determination). (Credit: Li, Wu, Johnson & Wu, 2011).[9]

And what studies have demonstrated is that psychological empowerment increases employee engagement. And it's linked to increased organisational success. It's also linked to a reduction in emotional exhaustion and burnout. So, employee wellbeing levels increase. While absenteeism reduces. Winning.

So how do you do it like Larry Page? Put simply, you focus on it, and you understand how important it is to have a psychologically empowered workforce when you're leading under pressure. And you do what it takes to help your team members find meaning, to have an impact, to build their competence, and to have self-determination in their role.

Hire staff with those things in mind. Do it like Google!

HOW TO BE AN EXPERT IN LEADERSHIP LANGUAGING

Leaders can sometimes forget the importance of their language. Especially when they're under pressure, which is when language is most important. It can be a serious game changer, when it comes to improving or negatively impacting a relationship.

A significant amount of my coaching work is around how to use languaging more effectively. And how to use language to connect more with team members. Recently, I was working with a senior manager, who was worried about having a conversation with one of their leadership team. The manager was worried that it was going to be a 'relationship-ending conversation.'

Only because the manager hadn't worked through (at that stage) how to effectively convey their message, in a way that was not triggering for the other person. Once we were able to talk through it, and talk through the approach, the manager was confident that the conversation could build the relationship, not break it.

The research of a friend of mine revealed that good leaders realise that 'individuals are a complex patchwork of social norms, cognitive conditioning, and personal constructs, which are all powerful in shaping a person's identity.' People's perspectives shape how they receive a message.

This is not to say that you shouldn't deliver bad news. Leaders have to. Regularly. It's so that you can deliver bad news with the right intent and get the right outcome. If you're committed to that. In the book Fierce Conversations, Susan Scott[19] explains that relationships are built on conversations. Conversations are the relationship. So, if you want a good relationship with your team, choosing your languaging carefully, and leaning into connection as well as direction, will help you, no end.

These top three things will help change your languaging and your connection—if you can nail them.

ONE HAVE MORE QUESTIONS THAN STATEMENTS.

Having bigger and better questions is the key to connection. When you're asking questions, it shows that you're more interested in the other person, and you're being more interested than interesting. It's very difficult to get to know someone if you're talking at them, not with them.

Asking questions is a skill set. It's simple, but not easy. It takes practice. The better quality the question, the better quality the answer, and the better quality the conversation. The thing about questions is that questions are the main skill of a coach. And leaders are coaches. All good coaches understand that questions are not just open vs closed, or direct vs vague.

Good coaches and leaders understand that the best questions are Socratic questions. The Socratic approach to questioning is based on the practice of disciplined, thoughtful dialogue. Socrates, the early Greek philosopher/teacher, believed that 'disciplined practice of thoughtful questioning enabled the student to examine ideas logically and to determine the validity of those ideas' (Credit: Wiki).

Thoughtful questions, like what people are experiencing. Why they think that's happening for them, and how they think they can respond not react. Other ways to use thoughtful questions is to start with 'which approach do you think we should take?', 'could we consider other options?', or 'would another option be worth planning out?' Thoughtful questions allow you to linger in the conversation. They allow you to find out more about the person that you're chatting and interacting with—and to get a deeper level of understanding about what's going on in the life of that human.

Even if you're not an expert at thoughtful questions (yet), asking questions is the most important thing in moving you in the right direction.

Develop the art of asking bigger and better questions, and then work on asking Socratic questions—to build a deeper connection.

TWO LISTEN TO UNDERSTAND, NOT TO RESPOND.

I couldn't tell you the number of leaders that I coach in the fine art of listening to understand. This is about not finishing sentences for others. Not looking as though you're just waiting for your turn in the conversation. Not having a pre-recorded script or a default response to ideas or opinions. And definitely not drifting off in the conversation in your head, until the other person has finished talking.

Listening to understand is the one big thing that you can do to value someone. If a team member ever says they don't feel valued, what that means is that they don't feel heard. They don't feel understood. And this is an easy thing to change.

My tips for you are to hang off every word. Literally. Listen with an open heart and an open mind. Be interested in what the person is saying. Find a way to engage your brain in the conversation and focus intently. Look into their left eye and connect. Paraphrase with 'so what you are saying is...' Or even linger in the conversation with silence to show you are processing information. Sometimes it's important to let silence do the heavy lifting.

The language that you want to use is language like 'help me understand', 'so what you mean is', or 'what's an example of that?' These statements (or questions, depending on how they are asked) are clarifiers, and they demonstrate that you're engaged, and that you do want more information before responding.

LEADER ACTION

Develop the skill of listening and clarification, so that you can listen to understand, not to respond—to build a deeper connection.

THREE THINK FAST, TALK SLOW.

One of the most important skills of good leaders, and good communicators, is the skill of being able to think about the emotional experience that someone else is having while you're in conversation with them. This is the skill explained by Daniel Goleman,[7] and it relates to emotional intelligence.

And social emotional awareness, and then social emotional regulation.

What that means is that you can understand what's happening for the other person, and change your tone, your volume, your pitch or even your language to suit the situation. There are times when you need to deliver bad news or challenge a team member. And there are times when you want to deliver good news and recognise a team member.

During potentially high-emotion conversations, your ability to be aware of emotional states and adapt to the situation to create more or less emotion is the highest level of communication skill that you can develop as a leader.

This skill is important because every word has the potential to be a trigger for another human. Triggers are things that cause an emotional response. Common trigger words include 'no', 'I disagree', or 'you're wrong'. The word 'but' (try using 'and') is a major trigger for a lot of people, but it's used frequently in high pressure situations.

Now there might be times when you choose to use words like these, but be aware that when people are triggered, they're not going to be at their best in the conversation. As a leader, try to choose words that are less triggering.

LEADER ACTION

Be acutely aware of the experience of others when they're with you, and change your strategy accordingly—to build a deeper connection.

Leadership languaging, and communication, is about asking questions, listening to understand, and thinking fast and talking slow. It's as much about connection as it is about direction—and it's what you need to be better leader for your team, especially when you're leading under pressure.

THE STORY OF THE KING AND HIS WILD DOGS

Story time. My favourite time, by the way. Love a good yarn, especially when there's a leadership message in there.

Now, you have a job to do, though. As I tell you this story, I want you to think about who you are in it. There are three characters: the King, the Minister, and the Dogs (yes, it's OK to be the dogs...not all the time, but for this story anyway). And you might have heard it before, but let me put the leadership spin on it, and add a psychological safety spin as well.

Once upon a time, there was this King that had ten Wild Dogs. He used them to torture and eat all his Ministers who made mistakes.

On this day, one of the Ministers gave an opinion that was wrong, and that the King disliked, and that appeared to be a mistake. So, the King ordered that the Minister be thrown to the Dogs.

Following the decree of punishment, the Minister said, 'I served you ten years, and you do this?'

And then as their last wish, the Minister begged, 'Please give me ten days before you throw me in with the Wild Dogs!'

The King agreed.

In those ten days the Minister went to the guard that was guarding the Dogs and told him he wanted to serve the Dogs for the next ten days. The guard was baffled. But he agreed to the Minister's request.

The Minister started feeding the Dogs, cleaning for them, washing them, providing all sorts of comfort for them.

When the ten days were up, the King ordered that the Minister be thrown to the Dogs for his punishment.

But when he was thrown in, everyone was amazed at what they saw. They saw the Dogs licking the feet of the Minister!

The King was baffled by what he saw. He asked, 'What happened to the Wild Dogs?'

The Minister then said, 'I served the Dogs for ten days and they didn't forget my service...yet I served you for ten years and you forgot all at the first mistake!'

The King realised his mistake and ordered the Minister to go free.

I know, right? It's a great story, and quite a deep one, if you get into it.

So, who are you in that story? And here's my leadership reflection on each of the parties, including where they started, and maybe where they ended, as a point of reference. You might be at one end or the other, or you might be somewhere in the middle.

THE KING

The King was not a great leader at the start of this story. The King's leadership team lived in fear. They couldn't offer an opinion, let alone make a mistake, or they'd be sacked, or even worse—ostracised from the team. The King was intolerant, lacked empathy, and was unable to listen to the ideas of others. The King hadn't been to one of the TGG Leadership Training programs, and hadn't learnt the skills of creating conscious control or keeping emotions in check, even when team members might not have a great idea that they want to share. There was no emotional intelligence on display from the King, who overreacted.

The King then transformed. Through a lived leadership experience. The King's belief systems and values were challenged (and changed) by being made to have an emotional experience, and one that meant the King couldn't feel anything but remorse for the Minister and a level of guilt or shame for his own behaviour. Let's hope that behaviour change was permanent, and the rest of the Ministers didn't have to live in fear anymore!

At the end of this story, the King was willing to be challenged. And to change his mind. That's Challenger Safety.

THE MINISTER

The Minister was a solid team contributor. Always offering suggestions. Maybe even an over-contributor at times. Maybe making decisions without all the right information. And due to that, the Minister's information maybe couldn't be trusted. And the King, having coached the Minister in the past to make sure they provided the right amount of detail, had made another mistake. Or offered a suggestion that was not grounded in a business case or with good data. In some ways, the King had reached his limit (certainly not a justification for the behaviour), and due to a lack of emotional control, the Minister was sent to the Dogs.

The Minister then transformed. The Minister decided to use his skills to 'manage upwards.' The Minister was thinking quickly and talking slowly. The Minister knew that if he could help the King to understand what it's like to be in the Minister's shoes, the King might just change his behaviour. And it worked. The King stepped into empathy.

But the most important part of this story is that the Minister had a new team to work with. Once the Minister had joined his new team, he worked hard to build relationships with the other team members (the Wild Dogs). The Minister turned up in service (in the right way, with the right intent), and was able to connect with the other team members in a way that meant they became a high-performing team and were able to work well together.

The Minister to was able to apply a new strategy, to learn from his mistake, and contribute to a better outcome for everyone. That's Learner Safety and Contributor Safety.

THE WILD DOGS

The Wild Dogs (aka, new team members) were not very inclusive. They were known as the team that no one wanted to work with. They were aggressive, abusive, and abrupt. They hurt each other at times, and they certainly didn't include new team members very well. They were angry. And it felt like you'd been ripped apart each time you had to deal with them. They had the reputation of being a mean and nasty team, who were hard to work with, and hard to deal with.

That Wild Dogs team then transformed. They went from being an angry team, to being a team that welcomed a new team member. They were willing to change their belief systems and values and be accepting. They were welcoming of new ideas, and they became willing to help each other and to make sure that the new team member felt accepted and valued. After only ten days, the new team was a high-performing team. A team that worked together towards the same goals and objectives.

This new team became friendly and inclusive, and they all worked together and got along a lot better. That's Inclusion Safety.

Who are you in this story? And why? Maybe you were one at one point, and now you're at another point. Keep up the learning—it's how you'll learn to lead better under pressure.

DON'T LET THE PRESSURE WIN

If leaders could only see themselves when they're carrying on like pork chops, and berating their people just because they can. It can look like the 4-year-old having a temper tantrum because mum didn't buy them a chocolate at the shop. Seriously...

But they can't see themselves. And you know what? They can't see the damage that they're doing to other humans, when they let the pressure win.

Letting the pressure win means simply that you've given yourself permission to carry on, to get abusive, aggressive, or abrupt. The three As, and you've given yourself permission to let your emotions control your behaviour, instead of your rational brain.

It's a choice. We all do it at times. The challenge is to demonstrate emotional control more times than you lose it. Don't let the pressure win.

Because when it does, and you react (from the limbic part of your brain—which is hundreds of thousands of years in the making, so it's very primitive), you tend to do and say things that you regret. Or that you need to apologise for later.

And that's the only way you will not let the pressure win. By having emotional control. And care factor for others—who don't deserve to be treated with the three As!

Emotional control is like a muscle. If you use it, it grows bigger and stronger, for the next time you need it. Emotional control is responsible for behavioural control—behaviour follows emotions. And the situational control follows behavioural control.

In short, as a leader, if you want to be in situational control, at all (or most) times, you can't let the pressure win.

In our leader coaching sessions, I ask the question 'are you in eustress, or are you in distress?' Eustress is good stress, and keeps you focused and productive. Distress on the other hand is you letting the pressure win.

Distress comes from the Latin word 'distringere'. Meaning 'anguish; grief; pain or suffering of the body or mind', from c. 1300. Sounds awful.

Treat it like a competition. Me in control: 1. Pressure: 0.

Think for a moment what the 4-year-old looks like. Don't think about your response as an onlooker (as we judge the parent, without knowing what's going on for them). Think about what you would do, or have done, if that was your child. What would work best? Shouting back? Probably not. Smacking? Probably not. Reasoning with them? Probably not.

The thing that I found worked for our boys (that doesn't for girls, I'm told) is to change their focus. 'Grandma's coming over soon, let's get home' or 'your shoelace is undone'. Will that work all the time? Probably not. But if it works even once in that situation, could it work for you? I regularly use the word focus in our programs, and coaching.

FUTURE FOCUS

The first thing to do when the pressure really tries to win is to have a forward focus. 'What are we dealing with?' followed by 'what does a better situation look like?' and 'how will we get there?' Future focused.

PEOPLE FOCUS

Next, consider putting the people around you first, not last. Focus on people, not processes. Engage, and engage some more. Ask for help. Ask for ideas. Rely on connection, not direction.

SELF-FOCUS

Finally, and perhaps the most important thing to focus on is your own ability to deal with stress and pressure. Focus on not letting the pressure win, by having boundaries. Hold yourself accountable for your reactions and commit to responding instead. Commit to keeping yourself in good shape, emotionally and physically, so that you're ready for the distress when it shows up. Focus on your personal psychological safety, and be the leader that people remember because you dealt with stress, not used it as an excuse to lose your !@#t. Because BOOM situations will come.

HOW TO COPE WITH PRESSURE WHEN THINGS GO BOOM

The human species has developed to cope. We have survived millions of years of catastrophic events. We have even survived when other species of hominids didn't. We are resilient, and we are copers. But what does coping really take, as a leader, when things go BOOM? How do you lead under pressure when bad things happen?

Firstly, coping is not about being resilient. During the BOOM event, you're not practicing resilience, you're practicing the skill of 'getting through it'. Dealing with it. Grieving through it. Managing it. Being resilient will set you up with the skills of being able to cope more competently with a BOOM event. In the moment, it'll help you to rethink the way you think about the pressure and the stress of the event.

Here are some tips.

ONE RETHINK PRESSURE.

In her 2013 TED Talk,[15] Kelly McGonigal shared some interesting research on the stress response. Kelly shared that it's not the stress itself, but how we think about the stress, that matters. I know right? Confusing. In short, if you think the stress and pressure you're feeling is positive, it'll help you be your best right now, because you'll be more focused and alert. But if you have a negative association with the pressure, you're likely to struggle to cope in the moment, and in the long term.

Rethink pressure by looking at it through a positive lens. Know that as a species, humans are designed to experience pressure. Pressure keeps us sharp, it heightens our senses, and produces cortisol and adrenalin so that we're ready to act (yes, fight-or-flight). Or focus on the task at hand. While we don't have to worry about sabre tooth tigers these days, the pressure can still be thought of as supporting us, rather than sabotaging us.

Rethink pressure to use it to your advantage. And rethink the pressure of the situation, so that you can cope during it, and get through it more quickly.

TWO RESTATE PURPOSE.

When you're in a tough situation that you're trying to cope through, reconnect to purpose. And restate why you're doing what you're doing, and why the current situation is worth the struggle.

Restating your purpose helps you connect with it. Remember that if you're leading a team through a crisis, it's important to help them to know that there's a bigger picture, and that their struggles are being directed towards an outcome that'll be worth the effort. Your purpose might be just to survive the BOOM event, or it might be to build the most successful business in your space, or it might be to choose to take the chances that lead to the change and growth you need.

When you restate your purpose, you start to get a sense of it all being worthwhile, and your emotional brain starts to relax and to understand that the thinking brain is in charge. And when reasoning is in charge, most BOOM events are manageable.

And remember that on the other side of a BOOM event will be a reflection period of what you did well, and what you could do better next time. There will be some learning!

THREE REJECT FEAR.

That's a big call, right? Reject fear! The challenge is, BOOM events create fear. Fear of what's going wrong right now, and the fear of the future. Think of COVID for a moment—the biggest fear that people had was what their future held. How would they earn a living? When would it ever end?

If you've followed any of my work, you'll know that I work with leaders to help them create conscious control. Part of that process is about being courageous. And having the courage to step outside of your comfort zone (which you'll be doing during a BOOM event) and to try things that might not work. To tell your team how you're feeling and what's happening. And to trust yourself and your team to get through this BOOM event.

Rejecting fear takes courage. Leadership under pressure is about control, care factor, and courage—even when dealing with BOOM events.

And especially when you're trying to lead through them with team members who aren't on board with what you're saying.

HOW TO TALK TO PEOPLE THAT DON'T LISTEN

When you're leading under pressure, the one thing you don't want to have to deal with is team members who don't listen. Team members that nod encouragingly, then do something else. Or that just don't seem to hear what the leader is saying, which ends up in miscommunication or quarrels about what was said. It would be so much easier if team members just listened. It can't be that hard, right?

This might be good for team members to read, too. Listening to your leader is important, for both of you. If you'd actually like a harmonious working relationship, that is.

In my experience, for the team member that doesn't listen, there's generally an underlying relationship issue. It's not really a listening issue. It's a trust issue, or it's a respect issue, or it's a care factor issue. If I interviewed the team member who doesn't listen, they'd tell me that they have an issue with their leader. For whatever reason.

The fact remains though, that leaders need to be able to give clear direction (task allocation), and the team member needs to be aware of what's required, so the work can get done.

So, as a leader, how do you talk to a team member who doesn't appear to be listening?

ONE BUILD A BETTER RELATIONSHIP.

As mentioned above, a lack of listening is generally not the obvious issue that it seems to be. And it depends on how it shows up, as to what the likely issues might be. Being a mediator, I sit between leaders and their team members when the issues get too big.

It's the responsibility of the leader to sort out the relationship. And to understand what is happening between the two of them. That takes, firstly, extreme ownership to acknowledge it. Secondly, it takes radical candour (real conversations) to address it.

Read some of the other sections that I've written already for ideas on how to build this relationship. The first thing that you can do as a leader is practice active listening. That's right. Just read that again.

If the team member isn't listening, it can be a sign that the leader isn't. Here's the psychology: humans have a habit of projecting. Projecting means that we blame others for their behaviours, in the same areas that we have a behavioural issue in. We project our issues and faults onto others.

So, if you want to build a relationship with a team member who you think doesn't listen, the first thing to do is to be a good listener.

TWO SET EXPECTATIONS.

The big thing here for the leader is that the leader needs to do task allocation. That's one of a leader's key roles, and team members that don't listen and clarify, or don't listen and follow through, can cause the leader a great deal of angst. And they cause issues for their team, and for their team's performance. For that reason, leader languaging needs to be very clear, and it needs to be quite direct.

The most effective words you can use as a leader are 'my expectation is.' Or some other derivative of that, with the word 'expectation' in the sentence. Setting expectations creates clarity, and it develops deadlines, and it accentuates accountability. When you set expectations, you allocate the task, you clarify the deadline, and you finalise the follow-up plan. Then you get agreement.

Then you follow up. If your directions aren't followed (for a period of time), it might be time for more formal processes or discussions.

THREE PARAPHRASE AND PUNCTUATE.

Providing positive reinforcement when team members do a good job would be the most underutilised leadership tool on planet Earth (or in the Aussie culture, at least). The second most underutilised leadership skill is leadership paraphrasing.

What I mean here is not about the leader paraphrasing something the team member said. This is about asking the team member to paraphrase what they heard. Leadership-driven paraphrasing is an important communication skill that needs to be practiced and needs to be perfected. It can be such an effective tool to ensure that the team member is clear on the task allocation and clear on expectations.

As a leader, punctuate the importance of paraphrasing, by practicing it regularly. Get into the habit of asking your team member what they heard. What they understood. What they commit to. And then watch your communication quality improve.

In summary, if you have a team member who you feel doesn't listen, become a better listener. Hear what they're saying, and understand if they have issues. Then, as part of your conversations, use the word expectation. Finally, use the skill of leadership paraphrasing, which is about asking your team member to repeat back what they heard.

Commit to learning these skills. They'll save you when you're leading under pressure—the most important time for your team members to listen to you.

ACTIVITY 1.4
LEAD UNDER PRESSURE

Take some time now to think about what you've learnt in the last chapter.

Answering the series of questions on the following pages will help you to learn more about how you perform in your leadership role when you're under pressure, and why. Alternatively, think or write about ways you could improve your conscious control and change your focus to be adaptive rather than reactive when you're in a BOOM situation.

Outline some of your emotions, and how you deal with them, when you're under pressure.

Can you think of something you could do right now to help a team member, or respond to them with more compassion?

Can you think of a BOOM event where you used delegation effectively? Or didn't, when you should have?

Can you think of any ways you could help a team member get more meaning from their work?

Can you think of any ways you could help a team member achieve their personal goals and objectives for their work?

Can you think of any ways you could show a team member how their work adds value to the organisation?

Do you think your team members feel confident and capable in their roles under your leadership? Why, or why not?

Do you think you're a good listener when dealing with your team? Why, or why not?

What ways can you think of to improve your future focus when you're under pressure?

What things could you do to stop reacting and start responding thoughtfully when you're under pressure?

SKILL V

KNOW YOUR LEADERSHIP STYLE

ONCE UPON A TIME IN THE WORLD OF LEADERSHIP, A BOOK WAS PUBLISHED.

It defined as succinctly as it could the difference between transformational and transactional leadership.

And what it meant to be a transformational leader. The year was 1978, the book was titled Leadership, and the author was James MacGregor Burns.[2]

Are you a transactional or a transformational leader? Or, let's go one step further, and add two other leadership styles to the mix, as there's a leadership style that sits before both transactional leadership and transformational leadership.

So, what's your leadership style? Remembering that transformational leadership is the nirvana of leadership, and that there are times when you might need to demonstrate the other leadership styles. On purpose, not by default. And with the right intent. Also remembering that under pressure, leaders can tend to revert to a 'lower-level' leadership style.

TEPID LEADERSHIP

Tepid leadership (a TGG descriptor) is about hands-off leadership. The leader who is tepid would describe themselves as having an 'autonomous' style. 'My team is self-managing,' they might say. 'They're all good at their jobs, and they don't need me interfering.' Yes, but they do need to you understand what is happening in the team. In a textbook on leadership, this style would be defined as laissez-faire.

TRANSACTIONAL LEADERSHIP

Transactional leadership is based very much on the exchange. Or a contingent reward. This leadership style is conditional, and you'll hear transactional leaders say, 'if only they'd do what they're supposed to, I'd reward them.' These leaders are very focused on process and procedures. They expect strict compliance with business practice and are on the lookout for variance or non-compliance.

TRUST-LESS LEADERSHIP

Trust-less leadership (another TGG descriptor) is about overly hands on leadership. Aka: micromanagement. The trust-less leader might say that 'if you want it done properly, you need to do it yourself,' or 'I have to keep showing people how to do their jobs—when will they ever learn?' Trust-less leaders miss getting the best out of their teams, as they don't allow them to shine and be their best. A textbook definition might call this leadership style an authoritarian one.

TRANSFORMATIONAL LEADERSHIP

This leadership style, in short, is about developing more leaders. Inspiring followers to achieve extraordinary outcomes for themselves and the team. In 2015,[17] Wendy Quinn described that transformational leaders focus on individualised consideration of each team member. They create intellectual stimulation, they provide inspirational motivation, and a role model of idealised influence. These leaders engage hearts and minds. Be one.

WHAT LEADERSHIP STYLE AM I?

I'm a good leader...now. But I wasn't, in the early days of my leadership journey, even when I thought I was.

I'm one of the 90% of hoomanz on planet Earth who aren't born leaders. I'm a bred leader. Through and through. The leadership lessons I've learnt— especially the big ones—were learnt in the school of hard knocks.

One of the questions I used to ask myself was, 'what leadership style am I?' Which is a nice question. Not a great question, but a nice question. A better question would be, 'what leadership style do I want to develop?'

Some leaders say to me in coaching that they're stuck with their style, and they can't change it. For them, they're one style, and that's it. Not true, but remember, if you believe it, it's real for you.

Leadership is learnt. If you're happy with your current leadership style, stick with it. But if you think there might be an opportunity to change or improve something, try that and see what happens. Upgrade your mindset, upskill your leadership, and uplift your teams.

But how do you develop your leadership style? Great question.

ONE GET BACK TO BASICS.

Now, at least 50% of my readership will check out after this paragraph. Tell you why. Because every time I use the word transformational leadership, our clients say that it's outdated, it's cliché, it's boring.

And it might be boring for you. But it's not boring for your teams, and your team members, who want you to demonstrate transformational leadership rather than transactional leadership.

Transformation leadership, in its simplest form, is about creating more leaders. Plain and simple. That means seeing the potential in others, being willing to develop them, and making sure they get the opportunity to shine.

As a team member, who doesn't want that? Just because you don't like the word transformational, doesn't mean that's not what's required.

Be transformative. Don't direct your team members (transactions). Be proactive (not reactive) and communicate for connection, not direction.

So what leadership style am I? Heading towards transformational!

TWO FOCUS ON YOUR COMMUNICATION STYLE, NOT YOUR LEADERSHIP STYLE.

Here's a thought for you—instead of trying to work out what style of leader you are, work out what type of communicator you are.

Something as simple as DiSC profiling can tell you a lot about your style. It can tell you if you're Dominant (direct), Influential (connected), Steady (facilitative), or conscientious (detailed).

And if that style is working for you, double down on it. If you think you might like to learn another style, do it.

High Ds or High Cs aren't great communication styles for leaders. There are times when you need to be direct or focus on numbers. Cool. But I can tell you that team members don't respond to leaders who are high D or high C. There's just no connection.

The big thing about focusing on your communication style is that you get to know yours, but you also get to know other people's styles.

Having done DiSC work for so long (and this is a bit of my weirdness), I categorise people when I speak to them into D, I, S, or C, and I try to tailor my style to theirs. Why? Because people don't want to be communicated with in your style. They want to be communicated with in theirs. Simple.

It's not what leadership style am I— it's what communication style am I?

THREE YOU CAN GET ALL THEORETICAL ON IT.

I'm theory-based hooman. I'm studying a PhD in leading under pressure, and how to help leaders stay calm during trying times. I spend my weekends reading research reports—no kidding. And I love it.

Someone asked me in a session the other day, where all of my knowledge retention comes from. And all I could say is that I research a lot.

There are very few leaders that I come across who could really hold a quality conversation about leadership styles. Which is cool. But I just think that if you really want to know what leadership style you are, go deep on the data. Unpack the research and the statistics. The way to do this is to put 'scholarly articles' at the back of your search in Google. Google will give you a list of research that's already been done on the topic. FYI: the words 'what leadership style am I' are some of the most searched on Google, in relation to leadership (see Answer the Public).

Most people would do a quick search and move on. But to really answer this question is a full day of research. Pick twenty research articles, and unpack them. Understand the research. If that appeals to you. If not, all good. Again, you do you.

My research has taken me through theories like authentic, conscious, and charismatic leadership. There's the Great Man theory of leadership (not really PC, but hey). There's humanistic leadership, there's trait leadership, contingent leadership, and there's even Machiavellian leadership (definitely Google that one). Even Adolf Hitler wrote a book on leadership. True story. I can't bring myself to read that one, yet, but it's out there.

Again, it's good to know where you are now. But it's even better to be heading for some leadership style that's more aligned with who you want to become as a leader.

So it's not what leadership style am I—it's what leadership styles are there? You'll find one that suits you. Then, go after it. Tell people what you're trying to achieve, and really, really, lean into that style.

One way to find it is with DISC profiling.

WHY YOUR DISC PROFILE IS MORE IMPORTANT THAN YOU MIGHT THINK

Fun fact: the same person who developed the character of Wonder Woman also developed DiSC profiling. I know—how cool! Dr William Moulton Marsten was a psychologist, lawyer, and comic book writer. He was also an outspoken feminist, and he developed Wonder Woman as a model of what's possible for women when they step into their power.

Prior to that, though, Marsten was focused on helping people understand and channel their emotions. It was groundbreaking at the time. And his book included a quadrant to describe the four different personality styles. At the time, they were called Dominance, Inducement, Submission, and Compliance. But these days, we know these four personality styles as Dominant, Influential, Steady, and Conscientious. Aka: DiSC Profiling.

WHAT IS DISC PROFILING, REALLY?

DiSC Profiling is the simplest and most effective way to truly understand how you operate, how you communicate, and why. It's a tool that unpacks your pace and priority at work, and it helps you understand your natural working style, as well as your adapted style (how you're adapting to be successful in your current role).

The process? It's a simple online survey, that doesn't take long to complete. We use DiSC Profiling with our clients, and include it in our two-day intensive leadership workshops, because it produces such an accurate and thorough analysis of their behaviour characteristics, and explains how dominant, influential, steady, or conscientious you are—and why. Our clients tell us they can't believe how bang-on their profiles are!

Let's quickly unpack the meanings of each behaviour characteristic. Dominant people tend to be very direct in their communication. Influencers are the salespeople, or those with high-level people skills. Steadiness indicates a preference to teamworking, and contribution. And conscientious people are the details workers, who like numbers, data, and processes.

BUT WHY IS THAT IMPORTANT?

DiSC profiling is important because self-awareness and self-understanding is the first step in any leader's journey to success. The phrase 'know thyself' has been around for a while now. And because DiSC is psychology-based, it allows you to understand yourself more deeply. When you unpack your profile with someone who's qualified to do so, they can give you an even more detailed explanation of the information provided.

On that note, please don't do your DiSC Profile unless you do unpack it with a DiSC practitioner. It'll create more questions than answers for you.

EVEN MORE IMPORTANTLY...

Not only does DiSC profiling help you understand yourself, it teaches you to understand other humans, and why they do what they do. This is the big winner, and where our groups get the biggest aha! moments.

The most important learning from DiSC Profiling is how to communicate with other people—especially others that aren't the same profile as you. Now that's where the magic happens! The space that it creates for you helps you to break down barriers, to get to know others, and to build better working relationships.

When you understand yourself, and others, your world changes.

HOW TO REALLY USE YOUR DISC PROFILE

We've administered a tonne of DiSC profiles over the last however-many-years, and it's one of my favourite leadership coaching activities to help people understand themselves and to understand others—and to understand why that's important!

But how do you really use that 30-something-page document, that tells you if you're Dominant, Influential, Steady or Conscientious? What makes it more than a report? What makes it the thing, the tool, that changes your life, changes your communication, and changes your team leadership? What you do with it, of course!

So, what can you do with it?

ONE READ IT BY YOURSELF.

I know this sounds straightforward. But most people don't. And this includes me (I am a high Influencer, and I don't have much Conscientious in my profile—aka, I don't do details and data). What I do though, is know the bits of the document that are relevant and that can move the needle for me. I refer to my profile regularly (yes, I use my profile in training programs—I take the attendees through my profile, to help me explain mine, and to help them understand their own profiles).

My profile is always in my computer bag, and it's never too far away when I'm doing one-on-one coaching sessions in case we need to refer to it. Not only do I read it, but I've internalised it, and I understand it. Yes, there are some parts of it that are 'vague', but I value the information, and I make it a priority to stay on top of it, and to keep 'knowing' it. Why? Because it's important that I do, as I not only train it, but I use it daily.

TWO READ IT WITH YOUR LEADER.

This one freaks people out. 'You mean you want me to sit down with my leader and tell them all about my personality and how to communicate with me?!' Ahhh, yep. Especially the page that's got the dos and don'ts on it. Just imagine for a moment if your leader is the type of person that'll take that information on board, and work on their communication style to better connect with you! Winner.

Now, I get that some people's leader might not be that growth mindset-focused and may not be as approachable as others. In general, though, if there's any chance that your leader is willing to take on board that detail and that information, have the conversation with them. If they ask why you're having the chat, just say it's to 'help you help me.' The idea of that conversation, obviously, is to set your leader up for success. To help them understand how to do great communication with you, and that if they step into the don'ts that you might be triggered and not do your best work.

It really is an amazing conversation to have, and one that'll really help you out. Mind you, though, if your leader is a good leader, nothing you tell them will be a surprise. If that's the case, that's outstanding. You're lucky that you're working with a great human.

THREE READ IT WITH YOUR TEAM.

This one REALLY freaks people out. Like above: 'You mean you want me to sit down with my team and tell them all about my personality and how to communicate with me?!' And again…ahhh, yep.

Especially the page that's got the improvement opportunities on it. Let your team know that you've been through your profile, and that you've reflected, and that you're going to actively work on one improvement area. You can pick more if you really want to, though one is enough. You might take your team through them all, but at the end of the day, this is about making a commitment to your team that you're willing to work on your personal development. And that you're willing for your team to hold you accountable to your improvement action. Now, don't say that you are, if you really aren't—that's not great for your credibility.

If you're doing a DiSC profiling process with your team, this is easier. Everyone has their own improvement actions, and if they're willing to share theirs, it creates some openness and better connection between team members, and between them and you.

As a side note: for the above actions, I have presumed (to a degree at least) that you are part of a psychologically safe team. And that your leader and team members are willing to listen, and to work with you on what matters to you in your DiSC profile.

Needless to say, the above actions can be reciprocal. Feel free to ask your leader to share their dos and don'ts, so that you're aware of them. Also, with the right intent, be willing to hold your team members accountable if they share their improvement opportunities.

Use your DiSC profile. Make it count. It's instrumental in discovering and developing your leadership style, and in your learning to be a better leader.

EVERY DAY IS A SCHOOL DAY... OR IS IT?

You learn something new every day, right? Of course you do. You wake up and learn what the weather is doing. You learn what's happening in the news, if you watch the tele. At work, you learn about what your team is struggling with, or what their goals are for the day. But is that really learning? Or is it just living, and passively looking for and listening to new information without internalising it?

Every day is a school day. But only if you're active with your learning strategy. And yes, learning is a strategy, and it's the number one most important thing that leaders can do for their personal development and professional growth. In our training programs, the first morning of our two-day workshops is about the L from the LEAD process (learning), and we follow that up with engagement, articulation, and demonstration.

For me, if you're waking up and learning, that's passive. If you're making your learning and your personal and professional development a priority, you're doing active learning.

So, what are the key elements of a being an active learner?

ONE PICK A TOPIC TO LEARN ABOUT.

Maybe it's just leadership in general, or maybe it's empathetic leadership or adaptive leadership or conscious leadership. Or leading under pressure with created conscious control.

Importantly, though, pick a topic that really lights you up, that you feel is not only important, but that will actually help you as a leader. The more interested in the topic you are, the more likely you are to be invested in the process of learning more.

TWO DEVELOP A PLAN AND A PROCESS.

This part of the process is about finding the process that works for you.

Right now the knowledge on the planet is doubling every 12 hours (crazy, hey?!)—but in 1945, knowledge was only doubling every 25 years. There's no shortage of information out there.

Here are some of the ways you can build an active learning plan (what you'll learn). Start with the topic you chose, then find a book to read. Watch some YouTube videos, read some research reports, or listen to audio books—turn your car into a university. Work out what will be easiest to fit into your life, and it doesn't have to be every day; every week would be a good start. Then, put the process together (when you'll learn). Is it in the mornings, instead of watching the news? Is it at night, before you go to sleep? Is it listening to Audible when you're driving? Commit to the process, and watch your learning go up!

THREE GET COMMITTED, NOT JUST INTERESTED.

Some leaders reading this have already started to think about all the extra time that this will take. *Anton, I am crazy busy already!* I know, I get it. But some of the ideas that I listed are not time stealers. They are actually NET (no extra time—like while you are driving) investments in time. Seriously. You can learn stuff on your drive to work and back. Easy!

Fun fact: we have had 20-year leaders come through our programs, and when I ask them what the last book they read was (on leadership or otherwise), they tell me that they haven't read a book since high school. True story. And that's not wrong, it's OK, they're still in leadership roles. We all have our own strategies, but if you want to understand your leadership style and develop into a better leader, you should be committed in your learning—even when you're crazy busy.

HAVE YOU NOTICED THAT WE'RE NOW CRAZY BUSY, NOT JUST BUSY?

As if being busy isn't enough, we're now CRAZY busy. Which I get, and I know the world is crazy busy. Most of our clients are leading under pressure. Whether it's the pressure of putting people over productivity, or the pressure of pushing performance, leaders are struggling to cope, let alone develop their leadership style.

And their teams are suffering. If the leader is crazy busy, the team members feel that. They'll sense the urgency, and the impact of the pressure on the leader. And more importantly, it's seriously hard to lead, and to create conscious control, if you're crazy busy.

Now this section is not about time management and helping you be less busy. I'm not sure that's the answer. I'm going to come at this section from a psychology perspective, and let you know what you can do to feel less crazy busy, which I think will help you more. In coming sections I'll provide some time management tips, but for now, let's talk about the psychology of being crazy busy (and how to not be...sort of).

ONE CHANGE YOUR LANGUAGING.

Here's your challenge after reading this: to not have 'crazy busy' on repeat every time someone asks you how you are. I know that'll be tough for some, because it really has become a default response.

Now I want you to change your languaging for the sake of others, including your team members. Every time they hear that you're crazy busy, they feel like they either can't approach you right now, or that they're not your priority. That's sad, right? Words have power in them, and they speak to the emotional part of our brain—the limbic system. Hominins are very intuitive creatures, and they pick up signals quickly and easily, especially through your language.

More importantly, change your languaging for you. Even though you're leading under pressure, and you're busy, find another response. One that feels right to you, and that rolls off your tongue. In response to 'how are you?', you could try:

- I'm very productive
- I'm happy
- I'm in control
- I'm all over it
- I'm getting it done

It'll sound strange at the start, but give it a try and see what happens. And let me know, please—I'd like to know how others respond.

TWO CHANGE YOUR FOCUS.

When you're crazy busy, you're focusing on all the things that you don't have. Like when you're lacking time, or some other resources. The universe has a habit of giving you more of what you asked for (aka, the book The

Secret), so if you're crazy busy, the universe seems to give you more to do. Regardless of your workload, try focusing on all of the things that you have got: think about how well your team is going, or how much they've achieved recently. Or how much you've gotten done. This one is a bit like me in the pool doing swimming training (which is hard for me, FYI). I always count upwards, instead of down. That is, in my head, I always focus on how far I've come (like 2k of a 3k set), not how far I've got to go (like 1k still to swim). It's such a great mental trick.

For me, the best tip I can give you on changing your focus is to get a gratitude journal, and start writing in it. Every day. If you're looking for some more information on this topic, see my radio interview with @The Pulse 94.7 recently (Robert Cameron).

THREE CHANGE YOUR PRIORITY.

Remember that this isn't advice on time management, it's advice on your psychology, your personal psychological safety, and your conscious control. Here's the thing: when you're crazy busy (or just saying you are), it's hard to be in control, and in charge of your emotional and psychological state. Being crazy busy elevates (heightens) your emotional state.

Here are the top three things to prioritise to help you be less crazy busy. The first thing is breathing. I know, too boring, right? But I can't tell you how many studies and how much research has been done on the power of breath. We now know that meditation (breathing exercises) changes your brain (read that again if you need to). 50% of the leaders I deal with tell me they either can't or won't meditate. That's cool. But try it. Just breathe deeply. Your brain is the biggest user of oxygen in your body, and without oxygenating your frontal lobes, you just don't think clearly.

The second thing is down time. Take some time to do some self-care. This topic has been talked about a lot, so another eye roll moment for some. But take this one seriously and watch your business change (or how it feels will change, at least). We take this one so seriously that all our coaching clients get some form of self-care as part of their coaching package (like a massage or movie voucher).

The third thing is to get more sleep. Sorry, too boring again. But get more sleep, and watch your emotional state change. I won't bore you with the studies, but some psychologists will tell you we're on the planet to benefit from sleep, not for our waking hours (there's a thought).

And if you make not being crazy busy a priority for you, in general, your mental state and the state of your team will change for the better. The workload might not, but how you process it will—and that's one of the most important things you can do to develop your leadership style.

My 28th Explosion Anniversary

I'll leave off this section on discovering your leadership style with an anecdote about my own leadership style development—and how it transitioned from physical safety to psychological safety.

At this time, 28 years ago, I was lying in the intensive care unit of the Gladstone Hospital, with most of the top layers of my skin blown off my hands and face. I was in the most excruciating pain I've ever experienced, and I was trying to understand what the heck had happened and why I was lying in intensive care looking like a French Fry.

Yes, it was only second-degree burns. Yes, I only spent two days in intensive care, before spending about five weeks in the burns unit in Brisbane. Having my skin forcibly removed every morning. By the most caring and compassionate nurses (burns unit nurses are really the best there is. They see and treat the worst of injuries, and deal with death and debilitation on a regular basis). Burns are a horrible injury. And that is something I hope I never go through again. Ever.

It took me about five weeks to recover and get out of hospital. I like to say that I was doing a five-minute job, trying to save five minutes, and I went home about five weeks later. And that was the crazy part about it. There really was no need to rush it. I had time, and the tradesperson working with me was certainly not pushing or trying to get the job done more quickly.

This was purely a personal or physical safety issue. Make a bad decision—which I did—nearly get killed—which I did. Suffer emotionally for the next ten years, trying to unpack why it happened, and why it happened to me. Which I did. I was angry with the world for a while. Until I took responsibility and ownership for the incident. My decision, my actions, my consequences.

About ten years after the incident, once I'd got my head around it, I decided to talk more about it (I couldn't talk about for ten years, it made me too upset, and brought back painful skin-removal memories). And memories of having someone take care of your hygiene for you (I couldn't use my hands).

Three things happened. Firstly, my wife and boys and I moved back to Gladstone (we worked around Australia for that first ten years) and when I got back, people wanted to know how I was. I couldn't avoid it anymore. Then, I was employed on a site where the induction involved watching the movie Remember Charlie. I was moved. His story touched my heart. Then, I got the chance to run a safety meeting. And to tell my story. Like Charlie did. And it was well received.

So, I quit my job, and became a speaker...much to my lovely wife's disgust. I was not acting like an adult, apparently. I do now, though, which is good. Love you, Mrs G.

After telling my story around the country and overseas, leaders started asking about how to keep their teams safe. My work went from safety to leadership. And safety leadership. And that journey that has helped me to really unpack what drives people to do what they do, and how leaders can lead under pressure, with conscious control.

Leadership training and consulting has seen me finish a business degree in HR and a science degree in psychology. It's seen me author five books, and read more books than I could count. And most importantly, I've worked with leaders and a range of industries, everywhere, to help them create high-performing and connected teams.

And my life has moved from personal and physical safety to psychological safety, the phrase that Amy Edmondson started to make famous in 1999.[6] Then, in 2012–2014, the internal project (Project Aristotle) found that psychological safety was the main reason that Google was able to create such highly effective teams. Since then, several books have been written on the topic, by Timothy Clark, Dan Radecki, and in 2019, Clive Lloyd[11] (titled Next Generation Safety Leadership). In short, psychological safety is about making it OK for people to share their ideas and opinions without the fear or ridicule, resentment, or rejection.

Personally, not only learning about psychology, but learning about psychological safety, has been the most intriguing and enlightening thing I have ever done. To be able to share with leaders what a psychologically safe team looks and feels like has been next level. My work has transitioned from leadership consulting—that was focused on the process of leadership—to work that's focused on the people side of leadership, on a deeper level.

And with a distinct focus on leadership under pressure, because it's during BOOM events (crises) that leaders need conscious control, and to really lean into care factor and courageous leadership. My work is emotion-centred, and people-focused, and helps leaders to understand why people, and psychologically safe teams, should really be their highest priority.

After 28 years, from an electrician getting blown up by a switch board, to working out that physical safety keeps people alive, and that psychological safety keeps teams alive (and helps them thrive), here I am. Hopefully, a transformational leader, who helps other leaders be transformational.

Living the dream.

ACTIVITY 1.5
KNOW YOUR LEADERSHIP STYLE

Take some time now to think about what you've learnt in the last chapter.

Answering the following questions will help you to better understand your leadership style, and ways you could improve it. Alternatively, think about ways to better manage your work schedule and free up more time to spend on learning the things you want to learn.

What does your DiSC profile say about you?

If you knew the DiSC profiles of your team members, how would this change the way you communicate with them?

What things could you do with your work schedule to free up time for more learning? What topics would you like to learn about?

Do you have a tepid, transactional or trust-less leadership style? What changes could you make to change it into a transformational style?

Think of some big mistakes you've made. What would you do differently to avoid them, or to better learn from them?

What things could you do to inspire your followers to achieve extraordinary outcomes for themselves and the team?

Is your languaging negative or maladaptive? What could you change about it?

AFTERWORD

If you're still with me, congratulations on making it this far. And thanks for finding me engaging enough that you decided not to put this book down and never look at it again.

What I hope has kept you connected to my words is the introspection with which I wrote them. I hope you can see how challenging your irrational fears and wrong beliefs helps you to stop procrastinating, to be a conscious leader, and to make time for real conversations with the people in your life you're trying to lead.

I also hope you can see how metacognition, and learning more about why you think and do the things you do—especially the things that aren't serving you in any meaningful way—can help you to find your real 'why', and to put away maladaptive behaviours (like procrastinating, and going BOOM when things go BOOM). Looking at your own personality and leadership style is the way to set yourself free to become the better leader you want to be.

This book isn't the answer to all of your leadership woes. But it's the beginning of the process. A process that needs to start from within, by understanding your own thinking, emotions, and behaviour. So you can stop doing what doesn't work, and start doing what does.

If you're an old-school leader, the one that I wrote this book for, congratulations on getting through a book you probably weren't very comfortable reading. See how getting comfortable with discomfort always ends up with growth?

If you're a new-age leader, the one that I wrote this book for, congratulations on getting through a book you probably thought was going to be a lot less work. See how facing the ugly truth you don't want to admit to—like team members who don't listen and don't respect your leadership—is teaching you emotional literacy, and improving your ability to lead under pressure?

There's a lot more to learn. Every day is a school day, remember? Go and get stuck into whatever piques your interest: metacognition; how to think fast and talk slow; how to have real conversations with people you're leading—or your own leader. This book is the beginning, and as long as you're leading, there shouldn't be an end.

Learn more from me. I have a bunch of books and a team of people who can help you become a better leader. Or don't learn more from me. Learn from anyone whose leadership is inspiring to you in any way. Or anyone whose leadership has caused you to not seek help when you needed it, or to feel unempowered, or to decide to never, ever lead your team like they led you. Go learn how to lead through introspection, and under pressure, and to have enough insight and conscious control not to go BOOM when things or people around you go BOOM.

If you don't remember anything I've taught you in this book, remember how it made you feel. If it filled you with hope and optimism, and overwhelmed you with the urge to commit to being a better leader, good. Go do it. If it filled you with dread and shame about how bad your leadership really is, good. Go get better at it.

Either way, you got this far because you're becoming reflective. You're learning how to think differently. You're learning how to react differently. You're learning how to answer the big questions—including why you're a leader, and why you do what you do.

Congratulations on finishing this book. You're upgrading your mindset. Keep going, and you'll be upgrading your leadership, and your team.

REFERENCES

1. Brin, S., & Page, L. (1998). The Anatomy of a Large-Scale Hypertextual Web Search Engine. *Computer Networks and ISDN Systems, 30*(1-7), 107-117.

2. Burns, J. M. (1978). *Leadership*. New York, NY: Harper & Row Publishers.

3. Clear, J. (2018). *Atomic habits: An Easy & Proven Way to Build Good Habits & Break Bad Ones*. Penguin Random House.

4. Cortes, J., Barragan, R. C., Brooks, C., & Meltzoff, A. N. (2012). Compassion in Children: Its Association with Prosocial Behavior and Aggression. *Social Development, 21*(2), 332-349.

5. Cotrus, I., Stanciu, M., & Bulborea, C. (2012). EQ vs. IQ: Which is Most Important in the Success or Failure of a Student. *Procedia - Social and Behavioral Sciences, 33*, 1105-1109.

6. Edmondson, A. C. (1999). Psychological Safety and Learning Behavior in Work Teams. *Administrative Science Quarterly, 44*(2), 350-383.

7. Goleman, D. (1995). *Emotional Intelligence: Why It Can Matter More Than IQ*. New York, NY: Bantam Books.

8. Lai, E. R. (2011). Metacognition: A Literature Review. *Pearson Research Reports*.

9. Li, J., Wu, X., Johnson, R. E., & Wu, J. (2011). When Does Employee Empowerment Lead to Customer Orientation? A Multilevel Study of Work Unit Empowerment and Customer Orientation. *Journal of Applied Psychology, 96*(5), 1191-1201.

10. Livingston, J. A. (2003). *Metacognition: An Overview*. Online Submission. Retrieved from https://www.researchgate.net/publication/234755498_Metacognition_An_Overview

11. Lloyd, C. (2018). *Next Generation Safety Leadership: From Compliance to Care*. Routledge.

12. Mackey, J., Mcintosh, S., & Phipps, C. (2020). *Conscious Leadership: Elevating Humanity Through Business*. Harvard Business Review Press.

13. Maxwell, J. C. (2007). *The 21 Irrefutable Laws of Leadership*. Thomas Nelson.

14. McCormack, C. (2011). *I'm Here To Win*. Hachette Books.

15. McGonigal, K. (2013, June). *How to Make Stress Your Friend*. [Video]. TEDGlobal. https://www.ted.com/talks/kelly_mcgonigal_how_to_make_stress_your_friend

16. Meng, X., & Sun, P. (2019). The Relationship Between Work Motivation and Job Satisfaction in Chinese Universities: The Mediating Role of Perceived Organizational Support and Psychological Capital. *International Journal of Educational Research, 93*, 1-11.

17. Quinn, W. (2015). Transformational Leadership: Confession, Discovery, Revelation. *Journal of Applied Management and Entrepreneurship, 20*(1), 21-36. Retrieved from https://wjquinnconsulting.au/images/pdf/Transformational-Leadership-Confession-Discovery-Revelation-Jan-2015.pdf

18. Sinek, S. (2011). *Start With Why: How Great Leaders Inspire Everyone to Take Action*. Portfolio.

19. Scott, S. (2002). *Fierce Conversations: Achieving Success at Work and in Life, One Conversation at a Time*. New York, NY: Berkley Publishing Group.

20. Willink, J., & Babin, L. (2015). *Extreme ownership: How U.S. Navy SEALs Lead and Win*. St. Martin's Press.

GLOSSARY

Akratic. Characterised by a weakness of will, resulting in action against one's better judgement.

Allocation. A consultative process of assigning tasks and responsibilities involving engagement, discussion and agreement between leaders and their team members (as opposed to delegation).

Amygdala hijack. Coined by psychologist Daniel Goleman. Where processing emotions such as fear, anger, and anxiety, overrides the prefrontal cortex, the part of the brain responsible for reasoning and decision making.

Avoidant-focused coping. A style of coping where the person pretends the event or stressor doesn't exist and avoids dealing with it.

Bandwidth (leadership and management). The capacity or limit of an individual or team to effectively lead and manage a certain number of people, projects, or responsibilities.

Big 3 leadership mandates. The obligations of leaders to the organisation, to the team, and to the self. Also known as values, transformation, and control (VTC).

BOOM Event. An unexpected serious or catastrophic event in the workplace or the lives of an organisation's employees.

Bystander effect. Psychological phenomenon where the inhibiting influence of the presence of others affects a person's willingness to help someone in need.

Care factor. Strategy for effective leadership involving giving team members time, using conversation techniques around psychological safety, psychological empowerment, and psychological connection, and being courageous in the process.

CBT. Cognitive Behavioural Therapy. A form of psychological treatment or therapy that focuses on changing negative or unhelpful thoughts and behaviours in order to improve mental health and wellbeing.

Challenger safety. One of the four stages of psychological safety in teams in Timothy R Clark's theory on how safe team members feel to speak up, and offer ideas, opinions, and views without the fear of resentment, ridicule, or rejection.

Conscious control. The ability to intentionally and actively regulate one's thoughts, emotions, and behaviours using conscious awareness and decision-making processes. Includes emotional, behavioural, and situational control.

Conscious leadership. A leadership approach that emphasises self-awareness, personal growth, and the cultivation of positive relationships and organisational culture. Conscious leaders are aware of their own thoughts, feelings, and behaviours, and how they affect others, and create a supportive, inclusive, and purpose-driven workplace.

C-Suite team. The group of top executives in an organisation (usually including the CEO, COO, CFO, CMO, CTO, and CHRO) who are responsible for setting the strategic direction of the organisation, making major decisions, and overseeing the day-to-day operations of the business to achieve its goals and objectives.

Dark Triad. A psychological term to describe three personality traits that are characterised by a lack of empathy, a tendency toward exploitative behaviour, and a focus on self-interest and personal gain. Comprised of three traits including narcissism, machiavellianism, and psychopathy. Associated with negative outcomes in personal and professional relationships, and in mental health and wellbeing.

Delegation. A process of assigning tasks and responsibilities to team members without collaboration with or input from their leader.

Deficit dialogue dilemma. A term to describe the challenge of effectively communicating and building understanding across different perspectives and worldviews in an organisation. Arises when individuals or groups with differing viewpoints are unable or unwilling to engage in productive dialogue with one another due to factors such as ideological polarisation, social or cultural barriers, or a lack of trust or respect between groups, leading to a breakdown in communication, a lack of cooperation and collaboration, and organisational dysfunction.

DiSC profile. A personality assessment tool designed to help individuals understand their behavioural preferences and communication styles. The DiSC model categorises people into four primary behavioural styles: Dominance (direct and assertive communication style and focus on results), Influence (persuasive and enthusiastic communication style and focus on building relationships), Steadiness (patient and supportive communication style focused on collaboration), and Conscientiousness (a cautious communication style and focus on quality and accuracy).

Disciplined courage. The courage you need to stand up for your position and maintain your commitments when things are going badly.

Duress. Wrongful or unlawful coercion applied by another person (usually a leader). Distinct from normal stress, strain or pressure.

EI (also EQ). Theory of emotional intelligence heavily influenced by Daniel Goleman. Applied in profiling tools to assess social management on measures of empathy, sensitivity, and appreciation; service, compassion, and benevolence; holistic communication; situational perceptual awareness; and interpersonal development.

Emotion-focused coping. A type of stress management that attempts to reduce negative emotional responses associated with stress. Negative emotions such as embarrassment, fear, anxiety, depression, excitement, and frustration are reduced or removed by various coping methods.

Empathetic courage. The courage to challenge your personal biases so you're better placed to experience what others are going through and to understand why.

Empathy. The key skill for leading under pressure. A process beginning with cognitive understanding of what someone is going though, and ending with doing something (where possible) to support them.

Golden Rule (of communication). Treating others how you would want to be treated.

Groupthink. A phenomenon that occurs when a group of individuals reaches a consensus without critical reasoning or evaluation of the consequences or alternatives.

Growth Mindset. A concept popularised by psychologist Carol Dweck. A belief that individuals can develop their abilities and intelligence through hard work, dedication, and perseverance, and that talents and abilities are not fixed, but can be improved through effort and learning.

High Reliability Organisation (HRO). An organisation that operates in complex, high-risk environments where the consequences of errors can be severe (e.g. nuclear power plants, air traffic control centres, and hospitals). Characterised by a strong safety culture, a commitment to continuous improvement, and a focus on identifying and managing risks.

Intellectual courage. The courage you need to turn your knowledge into action in the workplace.

Lencioni Model. A popular leadership development and team-building framework developed by author and consultant Patrick Lencioni. Provides a clear and actionable roadmap for building effective teams, involving trust, productive conflict, commitment, accountability, and a focus on achieving outcomes and results through both individual effort and collaboration.

LMX (Leader-Member Exchange). A leadership theory that focuses on the relationship between a leader and their individual followers or team members. Suggests that the quality of the relationship between a leader and their team members can have a significant impact on individual and team performance.

Manipulative Insincerity. Insincerity in your responses, feedback or praises, without the sugar-coating, that's delivered with the intent to hurt or harm.

Metacognition. Described as 'thinking about thinking.' How you learn and gain knowledge, and then how you apply that knowledge.

Normal Accident Theory. A theory the field of system safety engineering that explains why complex technological systems are susceptible to catastrophic failures or accidents. Suggests that accidents are an inevitable result of the complexity and interconnectedness of modern technological systems, and that no amount of planning, engineering, or design can completely eliminate the possibility of an accident occurring.

Obnoxious Aggression. Being clear, but not kind (also known as 'brutal honesty'), and unlike manipulative insincerity. Unintentionally causes hurt through poor delivery of the message.

Platinum rule (of communication). Communicating with others in the communication style they prefer, not the style you prefer.

PR6. The six elements of resilience developed by Jurie Rossouw. Includes vision, collaboration, composure, health, tenacity, and reasoning.

Problem-focused coping. Addressing the root cause of a stressor, and taking ownership and responsibility for either solving or minimising the problem with whatever resources are available at the time.

Project Aristotle. A research project initiated by Google in 2012 to study what makes a successful team. Identifies key factors that contribute to high-performing teams and improve team effectiveness and productivity, including psychological safety, dependability, structure and clarity, meaning, and impact.

Psychological safety. A concept describing the extent to which team members feel that they are respected, valued, and that their contributions are important, and how safe and comfortable they feel expressing their thoughts, ideas, and concerns without fear of negative consequences. Encourages open communication, promotes learning and innovation, and can improve team performance.

RACI matrix. A project management tool used to define and clarify roles and responsibilities within a team. RACI stands for Responsible, Accountable, Consulted, and Informed. The matrix is used to assign these roles to team members for each task or activity in a project.

Radical candour. A leadership approach that allows and encourages team members to share ideas and information, and contributes to the psychological safety of the workplace.

Ruinous Empathy. Insincerity in responses, feedback, or praises, and sugar-coating of criticism, to avoid the other person feeling bad.

Siloing. When leaders or team members don't operate as part of a team, but focus on their work, department, or business unit without regard for the rest of the organisation.

Senior leadership team (SLT). Also called Senior leadership group. A team of leaders of different levels that manage the running of the business to help it reach its goals.

Sunset-first approach. Letting the 'sun set' on a major decision or the execution of a major decision, i.e., thinking and 'sleeping on it' before coming back the next day to make a decision.

Systems Leadership. The practice of leading and managing complex systems, such as organisations, by focusing on the interrelationships and interconnectedness of the various components and stakeholders involved. Seeks to engage all members of the system in collaborative problem solving, decision making, and innovation. Requires a range of skills, including communication, collaboration, systems thinking, data analysis, and strategic planning.

Team Charter. A document that outlines the purpose, goals, roles, and expectations of a team so all members have a clear understanding of the team's mission, objectives, and expectations for performance.

Team management systems (TMS). A set of tools and assessments used for profiling and managing teams. Provides a framework for understanding team dynamics and individual preferences, and helps team leaders to identify and leverage the strengths of their team members.

Tell courage. The courage to articulate goals and objectives to the team.

Tepid leadership. A laissez-faire, 'hands-off' approach to leadership where the leader doesn't sufficiently support the team members.

Toxic Workplace Culture. An environment in which employees experience persistent negative attitudes, behaviours, and practices that have a harmful impact on their wellbeing and job performance. Common characteristics include lack of trust, bullying and harassment, poor communication, high levels of stress, lack of recognition and reward, low morale, and resistance to change.

Transactional leadership. A contingent reward-based style of leadership where the leader expects strict compliance with business practice.

Transformational leadership. A process in which leaders and followers help each other to advance to a higher level of morale and motivation.

Trust courage. The courage to trust team members to reach a goal themselves.

Trust-less leadership. Aka, micromanagement, where the leader doesn't allow team members sufficient responsibility and room for professional growth.

Tuckman Model. A widely recognised model in the field of team dynamics developed by psychologist Bruce Tuckman in 1965. Identifies four stages of group development: forming, storming, norming, and performing.

Try Courage. The courage to try and reach a goal despite the risk of failure.

Values, Transformation, and Control (VTC). A theoretical framework developed by Cameron and Quinn in the 1980s to understand organisational change and development. Posits that culture is made up of three main components: values, transformation, and control. Based on these components, organisations can be classified into one of four categories (clan, adhocracy, market, and hierarchy cultures).

360-degree survey feedback. A type of performance appraisal tool that provides an individual with feedback from multiple sources. Feedback is gathered from various sources, including the individual's manager, peers, direct reports, and customers or stakeholders.

5P process for facilitating workshops. Involves purpose (clearly define and share), process (how to run it and what resources are needed), people (who needs to be there), performance (facilitating questions, encouraging conversation, listening and documenting discussion), and polish (close out process to add value to the time the team has committed to the process).

7 states and traits. Skills for effective leadership that include learning, engaging, articulating, demonstration, empathy, resilience, and safety.

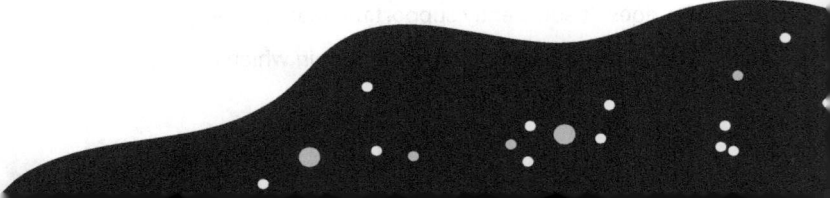

OTHER BOOKS
IN THIS SERIES

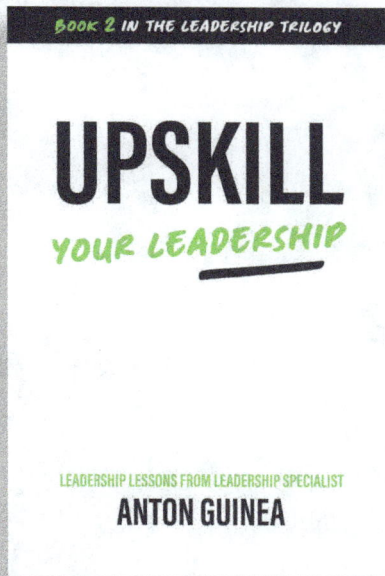

BOOK 2 IN THE LEADERSHIP TRILOGY

UPSKILL
YOUR LEADERSHIP

LEADERSHIP LESSONS FROM LEADERSHIP SPECIALIST
ANTON GUINEA

BOOK 3 IN THE LEADERSHIP TRILOGY

UPLIFT
YOUR TEAMS

LEADERSHIP LESSONS FROM LEADERSHIP SPECIALIST
ANTON GUINEA

Learn how to create conscious control, develop emotional intelligence, and operate with care factor to upskill your leadership.

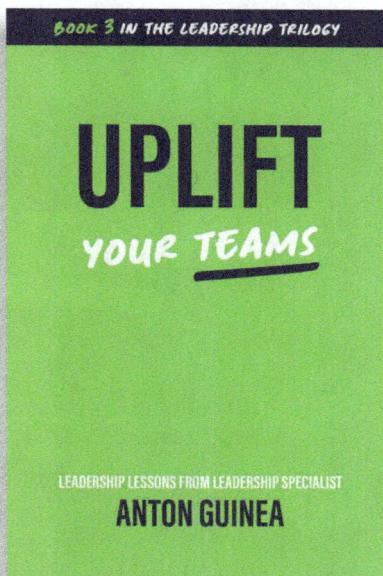

Learn the fine art of facilitation, how to deal with a team in turmoil, and how to use a radical candour approach to uplift your teams.

UPGRADE YOUR MINDSET

ONE-ON-ONE

Did you love this book? Did it give you food for thought—but leave you hungry for more leadership inspiration?

EXPLORE THE GUINEA GROUP'S LEADERSHIP TRAINING SESSIONS AND BOOK FACE-TO-FACE TIME WITH ANTON AT

ANTONGUINEA.COM.AU

◢ ANTON GUINEA

ABOUT *ANTON*

Anton's life and work experiences have led him to become a visionary thought leader, delivering the right mix of empathy and enthusiasm in all his programs. His energy, engagement, and enterprise thinking is helping leaders develop into transformational and inspiring role models, who uplift the people in their care, and create high-performing teams.

Anton is a widely regarded keynote speaker. But he is also a qualified Resilience Coach, and a graduate of psychology and human resources. He's supported by The Guinea Group team of professionals, who share his commitment to service and over-delivering for leaders and organisations within Australia and across the world.

This valuable experience, paired with his unshakeable commitment to his 'why'—leaving people better than he found them—underpins his truly transformative programs.

LOOKING FOR A
WORLD-CLASS SPEAKER
FOR YOUR NEXT LIVE OR VIRTUAL LEADERSHIP EVENT?

A professional speaker since 2005, Anton has worked with global organisations within Australia and across the world.

With a noteworthy ability to help people to think differently, Anton's speaking packages also comprise pre- and post-event support and resources, helping leaders and their teams to maintain their commitment to growth and development in the lifelong process of upgrading their mindsets.

Anton is a skilled keynote speaker. But he's also a researcher, and a former tradesperson experienced in working under pressure and for poor-performing leaders. This valuable experience, paired with his unshakeable commitment to his 'why'—leaving people better than he found them—underpins his truly transformative performance as a speaker.

To find out more about how Anton can help you to find your purpose, and to build a meaningful and rewarding career, visit us here.

◢ ANTON GUINEA